Chamber of Commerce brochure, 1943

On the Banks of the Wabash

Frank J. Martin

A Photograph Album of
GREATER TERRE HAUTE, 1900-1950

Edited by
Dorothy Weinz Jerse and
Judith Stedman Calvert

Photography Editor
Kenneth W. Martin

Indiana University Press / Bloomington

This publication has been made possible through a matching grant from the Indiana Committee for the Humanities in cooperation with the National Endowment for the Humanities.

First Midland Book Edition 1983

Copyright © 1983 by Vigo County Historical Society

All rights reserved

No part of this book may be reproduced or utilized in any form or by any means, electronic or mechanical, including photocopying and recording, or by any information storage and retrieval system, without permission in writing from the publisher. The Association of the American University Presses' Resolution on Permissions constitutes the only exception to this prohibition.

Manufactured in the United States of America

Library of Congress Cataloging in Publication Data
Main entry under title:

On the banks of the Wabash.

  Includes index.
  1. Terre Haute (Ind.)—History—Pictorial works.
2. Terre Haute (Ind.)—Description—Views. I. Jerse,
Dorothy Weinz, 1926– . II. Calvert, Judith
Stedman, 1940– . III. Martin, Kenneth W. (Kenneth
Wood), 1909– .
F534.T305 1983 977.2'45 82-47955

CL. ISBN 0-253-19035-5
PA. ISBN 0-253-20309-0
1 2 3 4 5 87 86 85 84 83

Cover photograph: The newly constructed Tribune building appears on the left in this 1913 downtown scene. The newspaper and publishing company occupied most of the space, but the third floor was the location of the Lease Brothers billiard hall. Before moving to this building, the Tribune Publishing Co. was located at 29-31 S. 9th Street.

*Dedicated to the Memory
of*
FORREST SHERER
1901–1979
Businessman, Humanitarian

Forrest Sherer was born near Kansas, Illinois. He and his wife, Hazel Holmes Sherer, moved to Terre Haute in 1920, the same year in which he opened his insurance business.

He gave much of himself to the community. In his philanthropic work, the youth of the area came first. The Boy Scouts, Gibault School for Boys, the Y.M.C.A., Indiana State University, Rose-Hulman Institute, and St. Mary-of-the-Woods College were all recipients of his leadership and generosity. He was an important part of Kiwanis, Goodwill Industries, the Wabash Valley Fair Association, and the Chamber of Commerce. His interest in the Vigo County Historical Society and local history is carried on in this volume.

Contents

Preface	9	Medicine	82
		Education	84
Serving the People	10	Cultural Activities	95
Wabash Avenue	14	A Sense of Belonging	98
"Crossroads of the World"	22	Leisure Time	106
Earning a Living	30	The Local Media	121
Reflections of the National Scene	54		
A Certain Notoriety	68	Photo Credits	125
Family and Neighborhood Life	70	Index	126

The Wabash River, which in southern Vigo County becomes the western Indiana boundary, has been important in the history of the people living in its valley. A route of travel and a source of both solace and inspiration, it is an enduring property of the ages; its flowing waters make no distinction between the generations.

Acknowledgments

Many have shared generously of their time, resources, and enthusiasm in the production of this book. Our gratitude and thanks go to

Indiana Committee for the Humanities

Forrest Sherer, Inc.

Vigo County Historical Society
Dr. William B. Pickett, President, 1978–1980
Joy Sacopulos, President, 1980–1982
Harry Frey, President, 1982–

Vigo County Historical Society
Editorial Board
Dr. Rebecca Shoemaker, Chairperson
Elizabeth Bevington
Charles F. Bradford
Judith S. Calvert
Brenda Christianson
Lois Harris
Kenneth Martin
Dr. Robert K. O'Neill
Dr. William B. Pickett
Dr. Edward K. Spann

Vigo County Public Library
Betty C. Martin, Director

Dr. William B. Pickett and *Dr. Edward K. Spann, consulting historians*

Tribune-Star Publishing Co.

The construction of the present courthouse, designed by Samuel Hannaford & Sons, Cincinnati, was completed in 1888. Funds to purchase the bell in the dome included $500 from the estate of Col. Francis Vigo, the early patriot for whom this county is named.

Preface

The story of the Terre Haute area can be told in many ways. In this photograph album the Vigo County Historical Society samples local life during the first half of the twentieth century. Some of the buildings, vehicles, and enterprises it shows are no longer in existence, and the material culture they represent can never be duplicated.

The photographs are valuable not only as a historical record of the fashions, architecture, and technology of the period but also as indications of what people living at the time wanted to record. There are very few views of the less-important buildings, the poorer neighborhoods, and the seamier side of life. Pictures of police raiding gambling dens or houses of prostitution are in short supply, just as the family album tends to show birthday celebrations and vacation trips rather than accidents.

Local history is a complicated affair. The memories of longtime residents and newspaper clippings answered questions as to "when" and "where" in the captions. An initial typographical error, copied again and again, can perpetuate a mistake indefinitely. At other times, differing memories and news accounts presented problems.

Space does not allow every facet of the community to be shown. We have attempted to achieve a balance among the various aspects of everyday living, and we are painfully aware that many important enterprises and organizations could not be included.

The majority of the photographs come from the files of Martins Photo Shop. For 70 years, two generations of Martin photographers recorded the people, places, and events of Terre Haute. Frank Martin founded the shop in 1906, and all seven of his children worked in the business at one time or another. Stewart was a commercial photographer, and Esther was a colorist. Willard and Kenneth purchased the firm from their mother in 1935 after their father's death. Willard managed the portrait department, and Kenneth was responsible for the commercial business. Willard retired in 1969, and Ken and his wife, Margaret, closed the studio, still located at its original location at 681½ Wabash Avenue, in 1976.

A continuous record of local history was developed at Martins Photo Shop. The completeness and thoroughness of the documentation is unequalled by any other collection. The photographs are a historical treasure of this century.

Garfield Purple Eagles at the state finals, March 1947.

1. The monument on the Courthouse lawn commemorates the "patriotism and valor" of Vigo County soldiers and sailors who served during the Civil War. The statues depict a cavalryman, an infantryman, a sailor, and a gunner. The monument was dedicated on May 25, 1919 during an encampment of Northern Civil War veterans.

Serving the People

POPULATION	Terre Haute	Vigo County
1900	36,673	62,035
1920	66,083	100,212
1950	62,214	105,160

County

Vigo County was formed by an act of the legislature at Corydon on January 21, 1818, two years after Indiana became a state. The county included parts of present-day Vermillion, Clay, and Parke counties.

The county is named for Francis Vigo (pronounced "Vee-go"), a Sardinian, who helped George Rogers Clark defeat the British at Vincennes in 1778–1779.

City

The plat of the original town of Terre Haute was filed for record in 1816 by Joseph Kitchell at Vincennes. He later sold his interest to the Terre Haute Land Company, which, in turn, persuaded the county commissioners to designate Terre Haute as the county seat. It was incorporated as a town in 1832 and as a city in 1853.

Terre Haute (pronounced "Terra Hote") means "high ground" in French.

2. A horse-drawn firewagon races to a fire about 1911. The drivers are City Firemen William Vendel and Otto Nattkemper.

Terre Haute Mayors, 1898–1950

1898	Henry Steeg (D)
1904	Edwin Bidaman (R)
1906	Frank Buckingham (R)
1908	James Lyons (D)
1910	Louis A. Gerhardt (D)
1914	Donn Roberts (D)
1915	James Gossom (D)
1918	Charles Hunter (R)
1922	Ora Davis (R)
1930	Wood Posey (D)
1936	Samuel Beecher (R)
1940	Joseph Duffy (D)
1944	Vernon McMillan (R)
1948	Ralph Tucker (D)

3. City police line up in 1910. The Police Department headquarters was located on the first floor of City Hall, at the northwest corner of 4th and Walnut streets. The building was constructed in 1874 to house the City Market, and was used for City Hall from 1877 to 1937.

4. Dolph Cross officiated at the ceremony on August 23, 1936, sponsored by Humboldt Lodge #42, F. & A. M., to lay the cornerstone at the present City Hall. Congresswoman Virginia Jenckes was instrumental in securing 45% of the construction cost from the Federal Emergency Public Works Administration, one of the agencies of President Franklin D. Roosevelt's New Deal. City Hall was one of a number of PWA projects in Vigo County.

5. Mayor Ralph Tucker, wearing his familiar white hat, accepted this street equipment in 1950. In its first four days of operation, the sweeper cleaned 148 blocks of paved streets. Formerly sixteen men using eight trucks could clean only six blocks a day. Tucker served five terms, longer than any other mayor in the city's history.

Law Enforcement

6. City policemen, Patrolman Edward M. Ryan and Lt. James W. Porter, work night duty on Wabash Avenue in 1946. Forrest Braden was Police Superintendent in that year.

7. County Sheriff John Trierweiler in front of the jail at 34 Ohio Street in 1946. It was the fourth jail to be built for the county; the original construction took place in 1882, and an addition and remodeling followed in 1908. This facility was replaced in 1981 by the Vigo County government and security annex building near 3rd Street and Wabash Avenue, just north of the Courthouse.

8. A test of this fire equipment took place in front of the present Courthouse in 1906.

Fire Protection

9. Ralph C. Dinkel was Fire Chief when this photograph of Station No. 5 and Fire Headquarters, 28 S. 9th Street, was taken during Fire Prevention Week in 1941. City fire protection grew from the first bucket brigade organized in 1816, to volunteer fire companies, and finally to a salaried fire department. The first motorized truck went into use in 1910, and by 1918 all the horse-drawn vehicles were retired.

10. and 11. Postmaster Curtis Gilbert moved the post office from Fort Harrison to the northeast corner of Ohio and Water streets in 1818, the first of a number of locations before the Federal Building, pictured above, was completed at N. 7th and Cherry streets in 1887. It was the first local building designed and built to accommodate the post office and federal agencies.

This building was demolished in 1933; the present building, shown under construction, was opened on the same site in 1935. Some of the columns and a pediment from the old building became part of the Chauncey Rose Memorial in Fairbanks Park.

12. In June 1938, Attorney-General Homer S. Cummings announced the selection of Terre Haute as the site for the medium security penitentiary for Indiana. Groundbreaking took place the same year on 1,200 acres south and west of Terre Haute along Highway 63. The prison employed 300 persons at salaries of $1,860 to $7,000 a year.

Wabash Avenue

Wabash Avenue, synonymous with "downtown," profited from interurban service and the greater availability of family automobiles in the first decades of the century. Farmers and residents of small towns in surrounding Indiana and Illinois counties, as well as city people riding streetcars, were now able to shop and bank in the downtown area. From 3rd to 9th streets, both sides of the avenue were lined with stores and office buildings. Wabash Avenue business prospered while owners of small-town businesses and country stores urged people to shop at home.

13. A turn-of-the-century parade marches east on Wabash Avenue. A group of small boys on the sidewalk march along with the band. The street has remained the same through the years, but the fashions, vehicles, buildings, and people change.

14. The 1940 Memorial Day parade approaches the city's busiest intersection—Wabash Avenue and Seventh Street. The Fairbanks Block on the northwest corner was still intact. Constructed in 1885 as the McKeen Block, it was razed in 1966. The ground is now a parking lot.

15. Labor Day has been an important local celebration since 1890. Carpenters Local 133 was one of the unions participating in this 1950 parade.
    Terre Haute has a long labor history. It was the birthplace of Eugene V. Debs and the center of railroading and coal mining union activities by the turn of the century. The idea to form the American Federation of Labor, predecessor to the AFL-CIO, was born in 1881 at a meeting held in the old second Courthouse—Empire Theatre building located on the northeast corner of 3rd and Ohio streets.

16. Looking east from the 700 block of Wabash Avenue about 1907, the viewer sees on the north side of the street Stuempfle & Welte's Washington Saloon at 8th Street and the Hulman Co. at 9th Street. On the right are the Varieties Theatre, at the southwest corner of Wabash Avenue and 8th Street, and the Ehrmann Manufacturing Co., makers of men's clothing, in the 900 block.

17. A traffic policeman operates a hand signal bringing S. 7th Street traffic to a stop in the early 1920s. The arrow-shaped street signs point north to Chicago and south to Evansville.

The Terre Haute House stood proudly on the northeast corner. The hotel building housed Gillis Drug Co., Yellow Cab, Beck Optical, Falber's Music, and Showalter Books. Next door the "chop suey" sign marked the popular King Lem Inn Cafe.

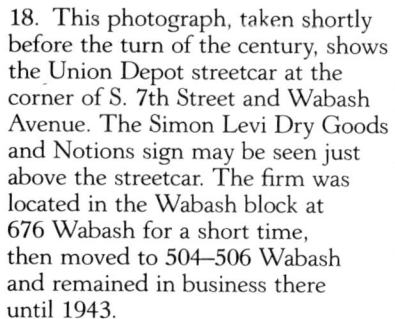

18. This photograph, taken shortly before the turn of the century, shows the Union Depot streetcar at the corner of S. 7th Street and Wabash Avenue. The Simon Levi Dry Goods and Notions sign may be seen just above the streetcar. The firm was located in the Wabash block at 676 Wabash for a short time, then moved to 504–506 Wabash and remained in business there until 1943.

19. Public transportation was in good order, and downtown parking was not a problem about 1920. Nine streetcars are on the tracks in the two-block areas shown here.

A 5¢ jitney bus on the Twelve Points run stands at the curb on the right, and an electric automobile is parked directly in front of it. A "fast" driver appears to be speeding around the corner, while the policeman looks the other way.

20. In a view of downtown Terre Haute, on June 22, 1925, we see the Twelve Points city bus in the left foreground. The horse-drawn vehicle across 7th Street is the City Street Department water wagon.

21. This picture, taken in August 1925, looks west on Wabash Avenue from 7th Street. All the parking spaces along the north side of the street are full, and not a horse-drawn vehicle is in sight.

The southwest corner of 7th Street and Wabash Avenue is occupied by the United Cigar Co. and "Patsy" Mahaney's confectionary. Among the tenants next door in the Kaufman Block are Frank P. and Wade Anshutz, dentists; Strupp Dental Lab; the Indiana Loan Co.; and Martins Photo Shop. The Crescent Theatre and George Carnegis, shoeshiner, share the 681 address.

By 1931 the theatre had closed, Scofield Optical had moved in and out, and John P. Chalos, father of P. "Pete" Chalos (who later became mayor), was operating a hat blocking and shoeshine business at the 681 address.

22. If walls could talk, the old Terre Haute House could have filled volumes. Constructed in 1880, the building is shown here in 1927, being razed to provide space for the new Terre Haute House pictured below. The Prairie House, built by Chauncey Rose in 1838, was the first of the three hotels located on this site.

23. Wabash Avenue parking was at a premium in 1939. The cars were on their way to becoming streamlined, and streetcars were literally running for their very lives. One year later the removal of the streetcar tracks at 7th and Wabash began.
   Six department stores (Herz, Meis, Montgomery Ward, J. C. Penney, Root, and Sears) were located in the 600 block of Wabash Avenue. Schultz and Smith's welcomed customers two blocks west.

24. South side of Wabash Avenue, 1930.

25. North side of Wabash Avenue, 1930.

26. The Christmas season was a busy time for shoppers and merchants alike. These shoppers were caught by the camera on December 16, 1947, in front of one of the two downtown S. S. Kresge stores. Other "dime stores," formally listed as "Department Stores—5¢ to $1.00," were the J. G. McCrory Co. and F. W. Woolworth—both in the 600 block of Wabash Avenue.

27. The crowd pictured above is taking advantage of the Dollar Day bargains in August 1941. Dollar Day originated in Terre Haute before World War I. Max Hammel of Herz was credited for conceiving this popular promotion.

28. A familiar sight each December in downtown Terre Haute is the mile-of-dimes booth, where members of the Optimist Club accept coins and bills to fund their program of clothing needy children. In the twelfth annual drive, in 1946, Anton Hulman, Jr., presents a check to Bill Shaker to help reach the $5,000 goal to clothe 400 children.

City officials and business people in Terre Haute, as in most other cities, have been plagued with the problems of fire, inadequate parking space, and keeping the streets clean.

29. Fire gutted Silver's Specialty Shop, a women's clothing store, on the evening of February 16, 1943. Through the years, Wabash Avenue has seen a number of fires.

30. Street cleaners are the city's unsung heroes. These two were at work one night in September 1946.

31. The parking lot is almost full and the gas pumps are open at an early hour on October 9, 1946, at the Central Park & Service operated by Sterling Pittman and H. Arth Collins at 660 Cherry Street. The buildings of Indiana State Teachers College are in the background.

32. Leaving downtown Terre Haute to travel west in 1948, motorists passed Gilbert Geckeler's Wabash Fish Market and perhaps stopped for gas at Fred Krach's Marathon Filling Station before approaching the Wabash River Bridge.

"Crossroads of the World"

Terre Haute was part of the history of river, road, canal, railroad, and air travel in America. Early settlers came from the east and south up the Wabash River and along the National Road—later known as State Road 3 and then in 1926 as U.S. 40. In the city it was Main Street and then Wabash Avenue. It became a coast-to-coast highway in 1935.

The north-south road was named the Dixie Bee Line—later State Road 10 and U.S. 41—becoming 7th Street in the city. It was the shortest route between Chicago and Miami. Since these two important roads crossed in the heart of downtown Terre Haute, local civic boosters began to call their city "Crossroads of the World."

The first train arrived in the city in 1852, and by the turn of the century there were ten railroad lines. Streetcar and interurban lines also served residents of the city and surrounding communities.

Gradually the use of automobiles, buses, and trucks forced the decline of rail traffic, but a new chapter in local transportation began in 1928 with the opening of air passenger traffic at Dresser Field.

33.

34. The old covered wagon bridge across the Wabash River was used from 1865 to 1903.

35. The construction of the present bridge, pictured here during the interurban period, cost $271,000. The dedication ceremony was held in 1905.

Railroads

Railroad trains, carrying both passengers and freight, have rumbled through Terre Haute day and night for more than 100 years. Terre Haute became a major railroad center, with the lines providing employment for local workers.

36. A conductor greets Margaret Hazledine, who was en route to Boston in 1908.

37. These employees are installing a reconditioned set of wheels ("retrucking") under one end of a box car in the local Pennsylvania Railroad car shop in 1947.

38. The Big Four's Duane Yards and Roundhouse, north of Maple Avenue and west of 25th Street, are pictured in this 1930 scene. The Big Four (Cleveland, Cincinnati, Chicago, and St. Louis) became the New York Central, Penn Central, and then Conrail.

39. and 40. There was a gradual shift from steam engines to diesel engines. These two photographs of the "Spirit of St. Louis" were taken just a few days apart in March 1950. The all-Pullman train made the trip between St. Louis and New York in 20 hours.

41. and 42. Union Depot, on N. 9th Street between Sycamore and Spruce streets, was completed in 1893 and razed in 1960. Will Rogers is credited with the quip, "Terre Haute has the only railroad station in the world with a silo in one corner of it." These photographs show exterior and lobby views in 1945.

43. The Big Four Depot at 7th and Tippecanoe streets was completed in 1899. The last passenger train stopped here in 1979. The Great Northern Hotel is seen in the background of this 1940 photograph.

44. Many famous and multitudes of not-so-famous people stopped at the two Terre Haute depots. Franklin D. Roosevelt was met by a cheering crowd of 4,000 at the Big Four Depot on September 13, 1932. Streets were closed and traffic stopped as he waved to the people and accepted flowers from the Vigo County Women's Democrat Club.

Interurbans and Streetcars

The interurban system linked farming areas and small towns with the larger cities. Local service was first offered in 1900, and Terre Haute became part of the largest system in the country.

In the city the interurbans used the tracks of the streetcar system. Mule-drawn streetcars first appeared in 1867. The system was electrified early in the 1890s and was used until 1939. Interurban service stopped in 1940.

45. The Terminal Arcade was designed by Daniel H. Burnham of Chicago for the Terre Haute Traction & Light Co. as the point of arrival and departure for interurban service in the city. Its ornate facade was created by architectural sculptors J. W. Quayle and Fred Edler. The building, completed in 1911, was also a streetcar terminus and later became the bus station.

46. Terre Haute Indianapolis T.H.I.&E. LINES and Eastern Traction Co. "Service to and from Terre Haute, Sullivan, Clinton, Indiana; Paris, Illinois; Brazil, Greencastle, Indianapolis, Martinsville, Danville, Lebanon, Frankfort, Lafayette, Crawfordsville, Greenfield, Knightstown, New Castle, Cambridge City, Richmond, Indiana and Dayton, Ohio." [From a 1915 advertisement.]

47. Chauncey Starkey (right) is the motorman on this summer car. A fleet of these streetcars was purchased early in the century for warm-weather comfort and pleasure.

Automobiles

49. and 50. The horse and buggy days were followed by the age of the automobile, which was destined to change the lifestyle of everyone in the Wabash Valley, including that of the Herman Myer family, shown here in their 1906 Yale automobile.

In 1901 there were 21 local livery stables and 13 wagon yards. Only two livery stables were still in business in 1929. In that year Vigo County issued licenses for 20,129 automobiles, 3,807 trucks, and 143 trailers.

48. Bowers Black and White Cab Co. became the Black and White Cab Co. about 1930. The office was at 709½ Wabash, and taxi stands were located at 8th and Ohio Streets, Union Depot, 7th and Wabash, and the Deming Hotel. They were advertised as "25¢ cabs," and four could ride for the price of one.

51. The R-V industry had one of its beginnings in Terre Haute when Warren and Ray Gilkison built their first camping trailer in 1922. Production began on a larger scale in 1925 at 1319–21 Wabash Avenue under the name E. P. Gilkison & Sons. The last of the Gilkies were produced in the 1950s. This Gilkie Travelier, equipped with innerspring mattresses, kitchenette, and refrigerator, sold for $285.

Buses

The development of bus systems depended on improved streets and roads. In the 1930s flat-nosed buses with rear engines replaced interurbans and streetcars in Terre Haute. Buses provided service to many localities that had not had any form of public transportation.

52. Two men rest in the shade of the Filbeck Hotel, 500 Cherry Street, in July 1947. The American Bus Lines ticket office was located in the hotel.
   The Union Consolidated Bus Terminal had opened in 1932 at 654 Cherry Street in the former Minshall home and Woman's Department Club house. The Terminal Arcade became the bus terminal in 1949.

53. Charles Turner began operation of the Wabash Valley Bus Line, one of the first intercity lines in this area, in 1921. The first buses were built by the Giffel Body Co. of Terre Haute on White Motor Co. chassis. Later the company was operated by four Turner brothers and one sister, and the name was changed to Turner Coaches, Inc.

54. City buses replaced Terre Haute streetcars in 1939. Mayor Tucker, members of the City Council, and traffic officers lined up for a photograph when 24 new 36-passenger diesel buses arrived in 1948. After much argument and negotiation, the adult fare was raised from 5¢ to 10¢. (Tokens were available at two for 15¢.) For the first time public transportation fares were more than 5¢ per person.

Airplanes

"If Terre Haute is to thrive and prosper she must look to the air for her future. The future of Terre Haute and aviation are linked together." These were the words of Mort Hayman of Terre Haute Airways, Inc., in 1928.

55. and 56. The Johnson brothers designed and built the first successful American monoplane in their father's backyard shed at 717 N. 10th Street. Louis, Harry, Julius, and Clarence took the plane to a field north of town on August 8, 1911. Louis piloted the craft, flying a distance of 30 yards at an altitude of about 40 feet. This success led to performances at carnivals and fairs.

The Johnsons' Terre Haute plant was destroyed in the 1913 tornado. Shortly afterward they moved their business to South Bend and later to Waukegan, Illinois, where the well-known Johnson Brothers outboard motors were produced.

57. George Casey, mechanic, and Harry Musick, local pilot, instructor, and manager of Terre Haute Airways, Inc., are shown at Dresser Field about 1929. Musick was later chief pilot for Eastern Airlines. The plane is a Curtiss JN-4D with 90 h.p. OX-5 engine. It was called the "Jenny" and was the most widely used training plane during World War I.

58. Passenger service was first offered locally in October and mail service in November 1928 at Dresser Field at S. 7th Street and Margaret Avenue. The airport officially became the municipal airport in 1930. The name was changed to Paul Cox Field in 1933 in honor of Paul S. Cox, a local World War I ace who was killed in a plane crash in 1932.

59. By 1940 it was obvious that Paul Cox Field would soon be inadequate, and plans were made for a new airport. In 1943 Anton Hulman, Jr., gave $100,000 for the purchase of 640 acres of land on east Poplar Street Road. Hulman is pictured here with a spade at the groundbreaking ceremony in August 1943.

60. The first air mail to leave Terre Haute from the new Hulman Field was loaded on to a TWA transport at the airport dedication ceremony in October 1944. Participating in the event were Harry Fitch, president of the Board of Aviation Commissioners; Anton Hulman, Jr.; Robert F. Prox, Leonard Marshall, and Ray Thomas, airport commissioners; Harry Mueller, superintendent of mails; Mayor Vernon McMillan; and Jerome Shandy, postmaster.

Earning a Living

Agriculture

From the pioneer days to the present, Vigo County farmers have worked rich productive soil watered by the Wabash River and its many tributary creeks. Early in the county's history corn, pork, and timber were the most important agricultural products. Pork has remained the largest livestock product, but in the 1980s soybeans have surpassed corn as the largest crop produced in Vigo County.

62. The picturesque Markle Mill was built on Otter Creek in 1816 and soon was the center of grain processing for the surrounding area. Two burrs, one for wheat and one for corn, were operated with water power. C. D. Hansel leased the property in 1911 and owned the mill when it burned on September 20, 1938. It was called Forest Park Mill at the time.

61. Steam-powered equipment was in use at this Prairieton farm in 1910.

63. Truckers and farmers wait as their tomatoes are unloaded at the Louden Packing Co., canners for Standard Brands, Inc., in 1945. The V-8 Cocktail was developed here and, along with other tomato products, it was produced locally until the plant at 2101 S. 3rd Street was destroyed by fire.

64. Davis Gardens workers here are picking cucumbers in the world's largest greenhouse in 1950. The firm was established in 1914, and 35 acres were under glass at 3300 S. 7th Street by 1929. The gardens produced and distributed cucumbers, tomatoes, and bibb lettuce from coast to coast. The business was closed in 1974, and the towering smokestacks were demolished in 1979. Westminster Village, a retirement community, was built on the site.

65. "Man may work from sun to sun, but woman's work is never done." The date and the names of the women are unknown, but this scene is typical of farm life in the early 1900s.

66. Farm wives and raising chickens were a traditional combination. Here Mrs. Harry Kessel is feeding her flock of pure-bred Barred Rock chickens in January 1949.

67. More Park, located east of downtown off Fruitridge Avenue, was purchased as a country home in 1887 by B. G. Cox, who developed it into a well-known dairy farm.
 Other well-known farms in the early 1900s included W. R. McKeen's Edgewood Stock Farm, just south of the present Memorial Stadium on East Wabash Avenue, and W. P. Ijams' Warren Park horse farm, located where Honey Creek Square stands now.

68. Don Foltz, Vigo County agent in 1949 and later director of the Indiana Department of Natural Resources, looks over the thoroughbred Duroc Jersey sows at the Kessel farm in Nevins Township.

Mining

Bituminous coal is Vigo County's most abundant natural resource. Small mining communities, such as Fontanet, Coal Bluff, and Blackhawk, grew up all around the county as railroads connected mines with their markets in the 1880s and 1890s. The mining boom in southwestern Indiana caused the population of the Terre Haute area to be at its highest in proportion to the population of the State of Indiana in 1910.

Production peaked in the 1920s. Conversion to less-expensive fuels during the Depression, truck transport, and conversion from steam to diesel power by the railroads following World War II caused the mining companies to lose much of their markets.

Strip mining became more economical than shaft or underground mining. The last shaft mine in the county closed in 1974.

69. Members of the miners' picnic committee line up under the image of John L. Lewis at their 29th annual picnic, August 10–12, 1945. A beauty contest for their daughters and baseball and tug-of-war contests for local union teams were held. Concession stands, carnival rides, and entertainment drew large crowds to the stadium grounds.

70. The "Doodlebug," a train transporting workers to and from mines west of Terre Haute in 1929, stops near Grover Station at Lafayette Avenue, about two blocks north of Ft. Harrison Road.

71. DuPont Snow Hill Mine #3, August 1945.

72. Walter Bledsoe & Co. mine at Dresser, May 1926.

73. Saxon Mine, Otter Creek Township, May 1938.

74. Maumee Collieries strip mine, 1933.

Business and Industry

75. Mercury, atop the McKeen Bank Building, presided over the business and industrial activity of the greater Terre Haute area from 1875 to 1958. Sometimes he saw growth, at other times decline. Natural resources, transportation, labor, management, changes in technology and markets, and the national economy were the threads woven into the business and industrial fabric of the area.

76. Wholesale grocer, Herman Hulman, 1831–1913.

77. G.A.R. Memorial Hall, the oldest remaining business building in the county, was built for the State Bank of Indiana between 1834 and 1836.

78. The Highland Iron and Steel Co., one of the industries secured through the efforts of the Commercial Club, employed 500 men to produce bar iron in 1908. The plant was located at N. 28th Street and 4th Avenue.

80. The Terre Haute Trust Company was organized in 1894. In May 1907, it purchased the Baur property on the southeast corner of 7th Street and Wabash Avenue for the site of their new building. Construction, as shown in this photograph, took place in 1908. In 1934, the company became the Merchants National Bank of Terre Haute.

79. The Terre Haute Savings Bank was organized and incorporated in 1869. It was located first in the Prairie City Bank building, 14 S. 6th Street, and moved to its present site, 533 Ohio Street, in the early 1880s. The building, pictured above, was finished in 1911. The top stories, occupied for a number of years by Levin Brothers, dry goods wholesalers, were removed in 1972.

81. The Terre Haute National Bank and Trust Co. personnel were proud of their newly remodeled building at 643 Wabash Avenue in 1928. It is now the main office of the Terre Haute First National Bank. The earliest limb on the bank's family tree was the Terre Haute branch of the State Bank of Indiana (1834). Almost a century of mergers and reorganizations led to the formation of the Terre Haute First National Bank in 1932.

82. This photograph of the Indiana Savings Loan and Building Association office was taken in 1904 or a little later; the first woman employee was hired in that year. The Association was organized in 1889, and was one of seventeen savings associations in business locally in 1900. In 1902 the office was moved from 22 S. 7th Street to the new Swope Building, where the rent was $25 per month. The Association now occupies its own building at 100 S. 7th Street.

83. Preliminary meetings to establish the Indiana State Bank were held in 1905 at the office of Dr. McClain. According to the minutes, "A few gentlemen interested in business affairs in the east part of Terre Haute met to talk over the matter of instituting a State Bank in the east part of the city." Property was purchased at 1211 Wabash Avenue, and the bank opened for business on June 16, 1906. This photograph was taken about 1948.

84. The Sycamore Building, still Terre Haute's tallest business structure, at 19–21 S. 6th Street, was erected in 1922 by the Citizens Trust Company. The Hansell Cigar Stand was located in the lobby, and Newlin-Johnson real estate, Western Discount Co., and the Monterey Land Co. occupied the ground floor in 1935, the year of this photograph.

85. At the turn of the century, the shop and residence of Henry W. Harrison, carpet and rug weaver, was located at 1306 Wabash Avenue. Pictured from left to right are Henry Harrison, Grandma Fuqua, and Frieda Harrison.

86. The Hudnut Co. began operations in Terre Haute, on the banks of the Wabash, in the 1860s. Corn oil (Mazoil), hominy grits, corn meal, and chicken feeds were some of the products turned out at the mill pictured here in 1914.

87. The address of the Fred J. Biel Cigar Factory was 409 Main in 1881 and 409 Wabash in 1890. Only the street name, not the location changed.

Note the wooden figure of Punch peering above the worker to the left of the door. Punch arrived in 1867, two years after Biel opened his business. He held cigars in one hand and chewing tobacco in the other. The carved wooden figure was wheeled onto the sidewalk each morning and back into the building for safekeeping at night.

88. The Standard Wheel Company began operations at the southeast corner of N. 13th and Plum streets in the 1890s. Part of the production of vehicle wheels is shown in a photograph taken about 1913.

The first Overland motor car was designed by Claude Cox at this plant in 1902. About 200 Overlands were manufactured here before production was moved to Indianapolis.

89. Ed Tetzel's welding and machine shop deals in guns, ammunition, sporting goods, and offers a "safes opened" service in 1941. The address is 315 Ohio Street.

90. Employees of the E. T. Hazledine Machine and Architectural Iron Works take a break to pose in front of their factory at 231 First Street. The company was founded in 1887 by Edward T. Hazledine, a master craftsman in hand-wrought iron who came to this country from England.

91. Someone's laundry would be ready to be wrapped and delivered as soon as these women finished the sheets and towels in 1925. The Columbian Laundry Co., 1112–1116 Wabash Avenue, advertised: "The Soft Water Laundry. There Is a Difference. Look for the Red Trucks."

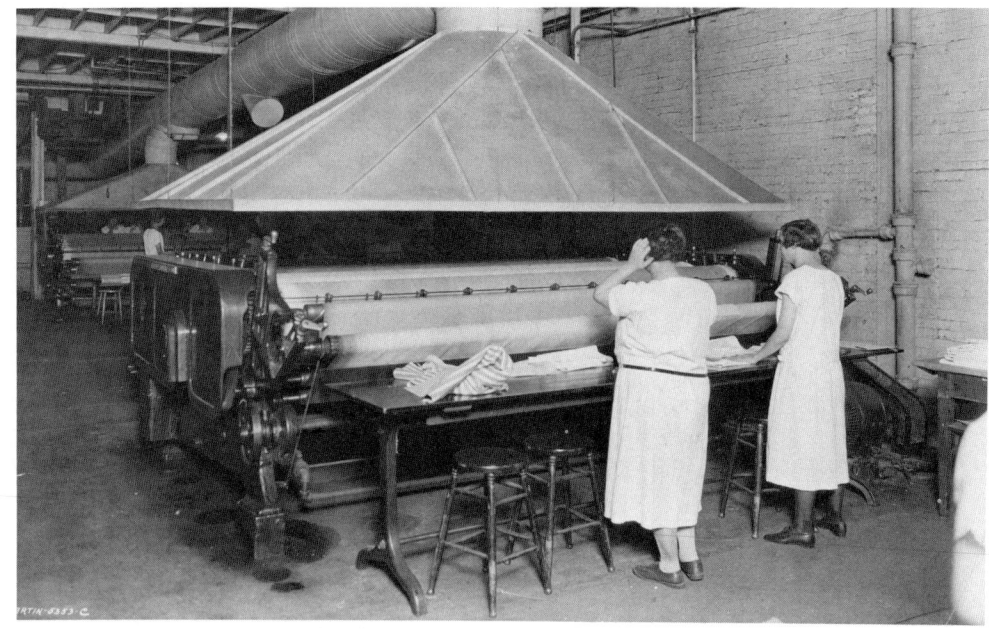

92. Ermisch Dyeing and Cleaning Co., in business since 1883, moved from the 652 Wabash Avenue location pictured here to 106 N. 7th Street about 1906. "Ermisch, My Cleaner" offered "Superior Cleaning of Ladies and Gents Garments—Sanitary Steam Pressing" in 1912.

93. If you purchased a piano "way back when" from W. H. Paige & Co., it may have been delivered in this truck. Paige's opened for business in Terre Haute in 1871. One of its 1915 advertisements offered "pianos, pianolas, and talking machines."

94. and 95. Root Dry Goods Co., 615–621 Wabash Avenue, employed 325 persons in 1915. Its delivery equipment included thirteen wagons and 23 horses. Some of the merchandise lines carried by the company were dry goods, clothing, books, house furnishings, china, glassware, groceries, pianos, and Victor-Victrolas.

96. Francis Hulman, a German immigrant, moved from Cincinnati to Terre Haute to open a grocery business in 1850. His younger brother, Herman, arrived a few years later to join in the enterprise.

The Hulman Block at N. 9th Street and Wabash Avenue, home of the Hulman & Company wholesale grocery business, was designed by Samuel Hannaford & Sons and opened formally on September 28, 1893. By this time Herman's sons, Anton and Herman, Jr., were involved in the business. The main building, the spice mill, and the liquor house were included in the block, shown here in 1931.

Hulman & Company's first baking powders ("Crystal" and "Dauntless") were produced in 1897. Three years later a new formula was developed and was given the name "Clabber Baking Powder." In 1923 the word "Girl" was added. The product became one of the leaders on the market after a national sales campaign in the 1930s.

97. and 98. Anton "Tony" Hulman, Jr., was only a few years old when he posed here with Grandfather Herman Hulman. He was to be the last male of Herman's branch of the family to bear the Hulman name.

Tony greatly diversified the family holdings and gave generously to cultural, educational, charitable, and religious institutions and organizations. His love of sports racing led to his ownership of the Indianapolis Motor Speedway in 1945. The words "Gentlemen, start your engines!" became his trademark. He died in 1977 at the age of 76.

99. In years past, a lady would not be "caught dead" walking downtown without a hat, and there were many local milliners to supply her needs. Frances J. Light and her employees pose in this 1915 photograph of her millinery shop at 713 Wabash Avenue.

Other milliners in business at that time were Sylvia Beasley, Ella Carter, Anna Chadwick, Elizabeth Cook, Louise Ewart, Minnie and Agatha Fortune, Margaret Kintz, Elizabeth Lincoln, the four Lynch sisters, Ada McLaughlin, Grace Swarbrick, Effa Tomlinson, and Margaret Wilson.

100. Customers are asked to "take a number" in 1945 at the Bon Ton Food Shoppe at 831½ Wabash Avenue. Established in 1921 by Charles Beal & Sons as the Bon Ton Pastry Shoppe, the business was later operated by Dorel L. Beal. It moved from its original location to 705 Ohio Street and then to this Wabash Avenue address, where specialty and gourmet foods, meat, seafood, and canned goods were added to Bon Ton's line of bakery goods.

101. The first shipment of National bicycles arrive at J. Edwin Sayre's store at 331 Ohio Street about 1912. Merchandise included motorcycles and sporting goods as well as bicycles. The George Hauck Fish Market was open for business next door. First located at 813 Lafayette Avenue, Sayre's moved to this corner in 1907.

102. Vitality Feeds are featured on this June day in 1942 at the Alvey Feed & Poultry Co., 127 Ohio Street. The sign reads, "87,000 Eggs Needed Every Minute—a gigantic task that can be done if your pullets are fed properly now."

103. A crowd of potential customers look over the latest model at Downtown Chevrolet, 120–126 N. 8th Street, in 1949. G. Harvey Froderman was president of this dealership as well as of Downtown Cadillac. Other new car dealers in business in 1949 included Adams, Cole, Dahl, Gasaway, Mace, Ranes-O'Daniel, Rodgers-Day, Shanks, and Vigo Motor.

104. A man pauses to drink a coke from the Coca Cola vending machine while attendants give full service to a customer at the Indian Refining Co. station at N. 7th and Cherry streets, in 1930. This was one of twelve stations operated by the company; the office and bulk plant were located at 2nd and Elm streets.

105. George W. Krietenstein and Herschel Glenn operated the Krietenstein Glass & Paint Co. at 30 N. 4th Street in 1922.

106. Fountain service was popular with downtown shoppers, workers, and students. The stools are filled at 7:51 on August 24, 1949, at the Gillis Drug Co. store, 6th Street and Wabash Avenue. Gillis had other Wabash Avenue drug stores, as did Baur, Doyle, Hook, Miller, Osco, and Riggs.

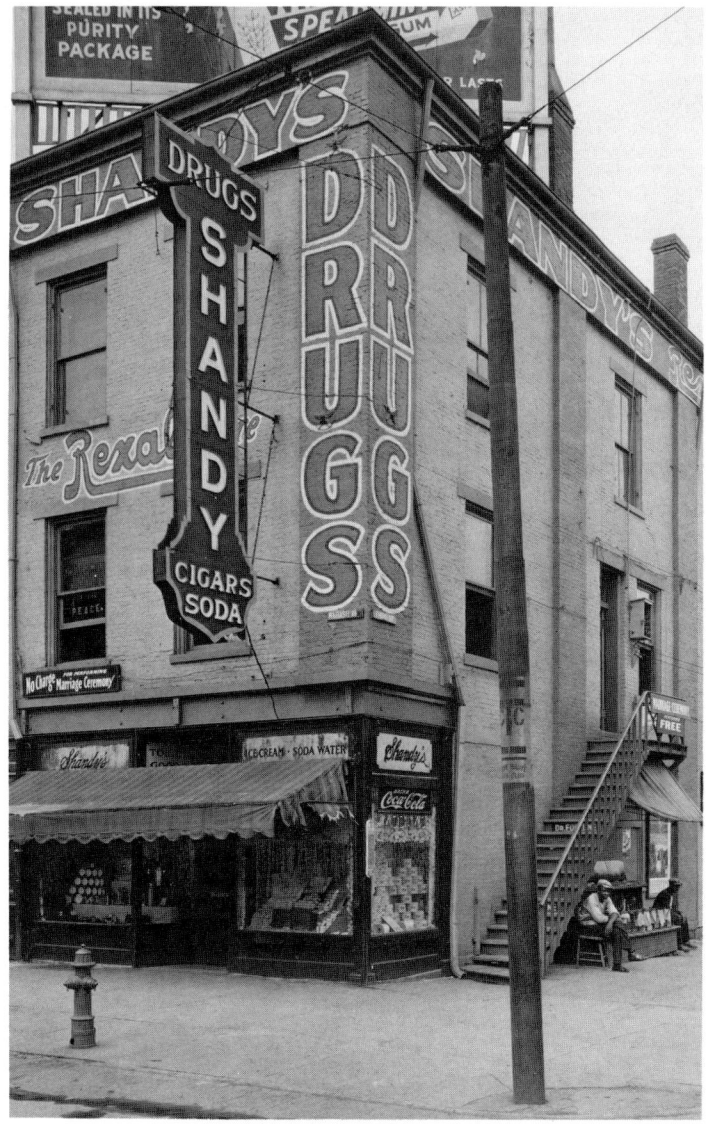

107. On a September afternoon in 1925, a couple could have their shoes shined at the stand under the outside stairway, have their marriage performed by a justice of the peace upstairs at no charge, and then celebrate with an ice cream soda at Shandy's Court House Pharmacy at 3rd Street and Wabash Avenue. Shandy advertised: "Drugs, Medicines, Prescriptions Compounded by Graduate Pharmacists."

The business was operated by the Gillis Drug Co. during World War II and by the King Drug Co. from about 1947 to 1957.

108. The city's first telephone directory (1882) listed 310 numbers, only 75 of which were residential. For some years both Central Union Telephone Co. and Citizens Independent Telephone Co. served the community. Businesses would list two phone numbers.

In 1920 Citizens bought out Central, and each subscriber was listed under a single number. Long distance calls were channeled through their switchboard to the long lines of the Bell Telephone Co., pictured above in September 1943. In 1956 Citizens was acquired by General Telephone.

109. Martins Photo Shop, 681½ Wabash Avenue, specialized in portrait and commercial photography. Stewart, Kenneth, and Willard Martin are shown with the equipment and vehicles in use in 1937.

The Martins pioneered many new methods, processes, and equipment in the Terre Haute area, including portraiture by electric light about 1910, flash-lighted group photographs without smoke, color photography as early as 1923, flashbulbs, and Dr. Edgerton's Kodatron electronic flash.

110. In 1943 Henley Bros. were operating sixteen large greenhouses at 2201 S. 19th Street. They remained open for business until the 1970s.

Local floral companies have supplied the community with beauty and color since before the turn of the century. Heinl's was established in 1863, and Cowan Bros. opened in 1894.

111. Employees of the Vigo Ice and Cold Storage Company, 100–120 N. Water Street, pose with their fleet of delivery trucks in 1932. Their advertising slogans included "Distilled Water Ice" and "An Independent Company."

112. John Barbazette, John and Robert McFall, B. V. Marshall, and W. W. Ray founded the Home Packing Company on N. 1st Street in 1907. Operations began with a capacity of 350 hogs a week, and by 1962, 8,500 swine were processed weekly. This photograph was taken in 1949.
    A powerful explosion on the morning of January 2, 1963 destroyed the plant and left sixteen people dead and 52 injured.

113. National Steel Corp. brought Stran Steel to Terre Haute during World War II to make Quonset huts, pictured here in 1949, for military barracks. The plant, formerly used by the American Car & Foundry Co., at S. 13th and Crawford streets, was purchased for the site of the new industry. A new plant, constructed on the same property in 1959, was closed in 1981.

114. These paint machines were in operation at the Smith-Alsop Paint and Varnish Co. plant on N. 3rd Street at the Big Four Railroad crossing in 1941. The business originated in 1909 at 104–110 Wabash Avenue and was moved to the present location in 1935. M. A. Bruder & Sons, Philadelphia, purchased the local operation in 1969, and the name was changed to MAB Paints in 1976.

115. The Bellaire Stamping Co. opened in Bellaire, Ohio, in 1871 and moved to Harvey, Illinois, in 1890. A line of their enamelware was named "Columbian" after Chicago's famous 1893 Columbian Exposition.

After the Harvey plant was destroyed by fire, a new plant began operations in 1902 in Terre Haute under the name Columbian Enameling & Stamping Co. The porcelain enameled steel products appear in this early photograph. The company became a part of General Housewares Corp. in 1968.

116. and 117. The Terre Haute Brewing Co. was incorporated in 1889. It was previously operated by Anton Mayer, successor to Mathias Mogger, who opened a brewery on the S. 9th and Poplar streets site in 1859. The name "Champagne Velvet" was registered in 1904 and became known as "the Beer with the Million Dollar Flavor." The brewery ceased operations in 1958.

118. The Merchants Distillery building, pictured here in 1939, was constructed in 1898 in the 1500 block of S. 1st Street. The plant was in operation except during Prohibition. Alcohol for the synthetic rubber industry was produced there during World War II. The operation shut down during the 1950s, and the building was gutted by fire in 1972.

119. Chapman Root stops to inspect an automatic glass-blowing machine at the Root Glass Co. plant, where the original Coca Cola bottle was designed and manufactured. The company, in business since the 1890s, sold the plant at S. 3rd and Voorhees streets to Owen-Illinois Glass Co. in 1932. Successive owners have included Wheaton Glass, American-Wheaton Glass, American Can, and Midland Glass.

120. Progress on the construction of the American Can Co. plant on the Wabash River at Sycamore Street is continuing in September 1932. Metal containers were produced at the facility, which was purchased by the Pillsbury Co. in 1963.

121. The Terre Haute Gravel Company site is covered with a December snowfall in this 1942 photograph. The company produced and shipped washed sand and gravel from its operation at 34th Street and Ft. Harrison Road. The daily capacity in 1942 was 3,500 tons.

122. In 1929 this site, at N. 10th and Chestnut streets, was occupied by one of seven branches of Western Indiana Gravel Co. The Union Depot tower may be seen in the distance. The location became the home of the Terre Haute Concrete Supply Corp. in 1944.

123. The Terre Haute Vitrified Brick Works, West Terre Haute, was founded in 1894. The company soon expanded from its original line of paving bricks to bricks for other purposes. A 1915 advertisement read: "No excuse for damp cellars and walls or unattractive buildings for Vitrified Brick will make your own home a health resort."

124. Coke is being unloaded from the oven into a conveyor car in this 1948 scene at the Indiana Gas & Chemical Corp. Organized by Alfred M. Ogle as the Indiana Coke and Gas Co. in 1915, the plant began operation at S. 13th and Hulman streets in 1916. Products are coke, gas, and other by-products of bituminous coal.

125. An employee of Terre Haute Malleable is finishing a rough casting in 1937. A. W. Wagner and H. A. Wanner founded the company in 1906 on its present site—35 acres on N. 19th Street extending north to Maple Avenue.

126. In 1942, Gartland Foundry Co. employees draw molten iron from the furnace to produce castings. The company, founded in 1904, remains in operation at the same site, S. 4th and Grant streets.

127. A stack of boiler sections are shown in this early photograph of the Frank Prox Co., founded in 1875. Cast iron heating boilers and mining equipment continue to be produced at the plant on S. 1st Street.

128. Construction is progressing on the Pfizer Co. plant on the site of the Vigo Ordinance installation south of the city in October 1949. This operation became a significant addition to the local economy.

129. The lights shone brightly in the 1930s at the Quaker Maid plant. A division of the Great Atlantic & Pacific Tea Co., the industry engaged in the manufacture of Ann Page food products from 1930 to 1979.

130. Commercial Solvents Co. was organized in 1919; the Terre Haute facilities, once used by the federal government to produce acetone, were acquired for the operation. One of the first products was Butanol, an essential ingredient of fast-drying lacquer. Grain was used in large quantities; a delivery in 1923 is shown here.

In 1943 CSC built, in record time, a large penicillin plant and was the first to produce that product on a large scale. CSC became part of International Minerals & Chemical Corp. in 1976.

131. Anton "Tony" Hulman, Jr., cuts his birthday cake at a Chamber of Commerce luncheon at the Terre Haute House in February 1946.

The Terre Haute Chamber of Commerce was the successor to the Commercial Club of Terre Haute. In 1915 it was said that the organization had more individual memberships in relation to population than any other Chamber in Indiana, and, with the exception of Dayton, Ohio, in the entire country.

Reflections of the National Scene

The conditions of the nation were reflected in the Terre Haute area as they were in all American communities. During the first half of the century, two world wars were translated locally into wounded, missing, and dead loved ones, as well as into increased prosperity in business and industry, rationing, and a myriad of war efforts on the home front.

"Terre Haute Saloons Pass into History" was the front page headline of the April 3, 1918 issue of the Terre Haute *Tribune*. Local brewery workers lost their jobs, and illegal drinking brought forth such popular tunes as "Everybody Wants a Key to My Cellar."

Union organizer Eugene V. Debs became the most prominent Terre Hautean on the national scene during the first quarter of this century. He was a spectacular campaigner; he ran for President on the Socialist ticket five times. Crowds greeted his Red Special train at depots all over the country during the 1908 campaign.

Terre Haute Ku Klux Klan activity was at its height in 1923 and 1924. The State of Indiana led in Ku Klux Klan membership during the early 1920s, under the ambitious leadership of David Stephenson. The Klan's early attacks on Blacks expanded to acts against Roman Catholic, Jewish, and foreign peoples. The local Klan home was located at 1501 N. 13th Street.

Between Black Tuesday, the 1929 crash of the stock market, and the beginning of World War II, the nation and the world suffered with the Great Depression. The General Strike in 1935 and the visit of U.S. Communist Party leader Earl Browder in 1936 brought Terre Haute into the national headlines.

132. Men from each branch of the military on the roof of the Post Office, August 1950.

World War I

Two shots fired on June 28, 1914 in the faraway Austrian province of Bosnia became the fatal announcement of World War I. By fall the European Central Powers were at war with the Allies.

The United States entered the war on April 6, 1917, sending its doughboys "Over There" to "make the world safe for democracy." The armistice was signed on November 11, 1918. By then 83 of Vigo County's young men had been killed in action.

133. Local men were urged to avoid conscription by enlisting at this recruiting station.

135. Eugene V. Debs was born at 457 N. 4th Street in 1855. His boyhood home was the Debs grocery at 11th Street and Wabash Avenue. His labor union activities began when he was nineteen with the Brotherhood of Locomotive Firemen, and nineteen years later he organized the first industrial union, the American Railway Union.

Debs served as Terre Haute city clerk and as state representative to the Indiana General Assembly. He was the presidential candidate of the Socialist Party in 1900, 1904, 1908, 1912, and 1920. The last campaign was conducted from an Atlanta prison, to which he was sentenced for making an antiwar speech in 1918.

Debs returned home in poor health in 1921 and died in Chicago in 1926. Many reforms that he advocated, such as the eight-hour day, pension plans, and workman's compensation, were later adopted by Congress. His home at 451 N. 8th Street is maintained as a state and national historic site by the Eugene V. Debs Foundation.

134. P.F.C. Harry E. Fitch returned home to serve many terms on the Board of Aviation Commissioners, amassing a large collection of local aviation history.

136. Men in uniform stand at attention in front of the main entrance of Rose Polytechnic Institute at N. 13th and Locust streets.

137. Crowds of Vigo County residents turned out to welcome returning servicemen at Union Depot.

138. Vigo County revealed the strength of its patriotism by oversubscribing its quota of four Liberty Loan issues and one Victory Loan issue of government bonds to help finance the war. James S. Royse, president of the Terre Haute Trust Company, was chairman of the bond sales committee.

139. A group of local residents interested in forming the Terre Haute Chapter of the American Red Cross petitioned for a charter in 1916. In 1917 the constitution was adopted, and work began at once.
    The needlework department made and shipped 24 boxes of hospital supplies for war relief in 1917 and 26,176 garments in 1918. The department had 22 working units within the county, one of which is pictured here.

140. Terre Haute was proud of its boys who fought in World War I, the "War to End All Wars." A victory arch was constructed in their honor at 8th Street and Wabash Avenue.

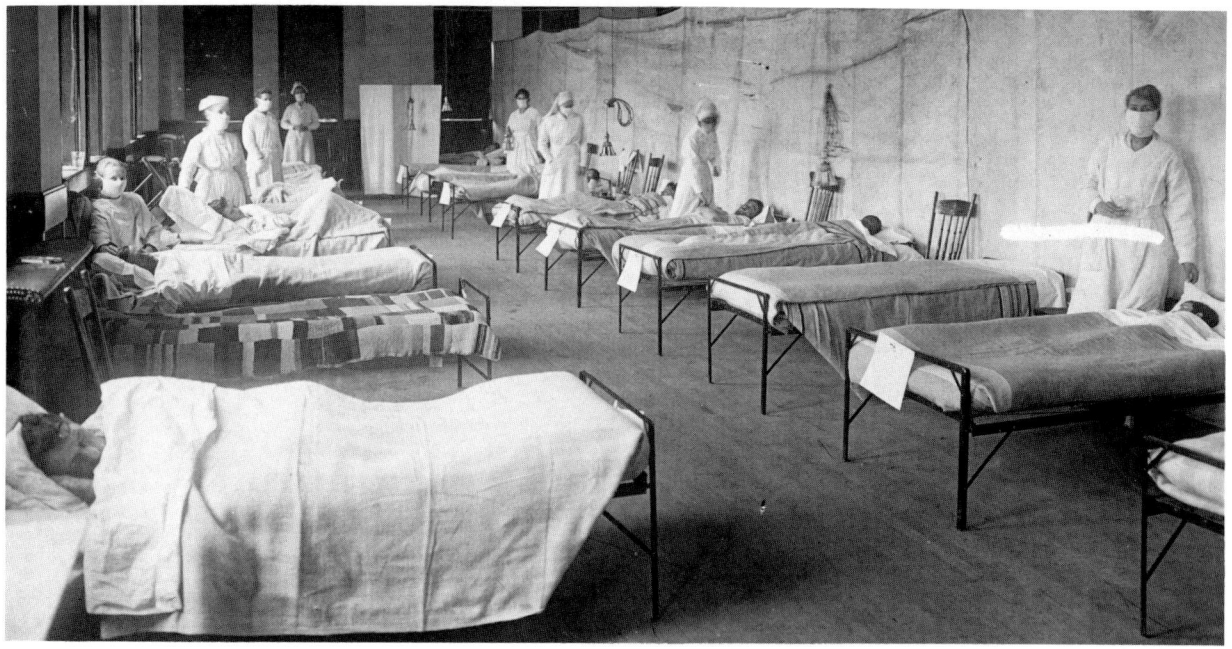

141. Near the end of the war a Spanish influenza epidemic swept the world and peaked in October 1918. In Vigo County, 246 persons died from influenza during the last three months of the year. Emergency facilities were set up in various places throughout the city and county to relieve the overcrowded hospitals. The Indiana Board of Health ordered that churches, theatres, schools, and other public meeting places be closed.

Prohibition

Indiana's statewide Prohibition legislation became law in 1917, and three years later the federal Prohibition Amendment went into effect. Amendment 18, repealing Prohibition, was approved by 36 states by December 5, 1933, calling the end to the "noble experiment."

143. Spots like Ed Light's Saloon, 313 N. 3rd Street, were destined to go out of business or "underground" when Prohibition became law in 1917.

142. Just months before Repeal, federal officers raided a still in a brick building midway between N. 7th and 13th streets on Haythorne Avenue. It was described as the best-equipped moonshine still ever found in Indiana.

144. There was good reason to celebrate at the Terre Haute Brewing Company when Prohibition was repealed.

The Great Depression

The 1930s were the lean years, the decade of the Great Depression. President Herbert Hoover was unable to carry out his promises of "a chicken in every pot" and "two cars in every garage." Instead it was a time of hunger, unemployment, and shanty towns called "Hoovervilles."

President Franklin D. Roosevelt took office in 1933 and the "New Deal" was under way. The alphabet soup of federal agencies, such as the CCC, WPA, PWA, HOLC, AAA, and NRA, brought action into the economy and relief to the impoverished. The American government was now in the social welfare business.

145. The building of the Chauncey Rose Memorial in Fairbanks Park, using columns from the old post office, was one of the local projects funded by the PWA. Among the other federally funded projects were: City Hall, Vigo County Infirmary, Colored Orphans Home, Riley Township School Building, Dresser School Building, Indiana State Teachers College Laboratory School, Indiana State Teachers College Commerce Building, Indiana State Teachers College Fine Arts Building, Indiana State Teachers College Student Union, West Terre Haute Auditorium, Number 2 Fire Station, Paul Dresser Memorial, and Garfield High School Gymnasium.

146. The blue eagle of the NRA is about to be fastened to City Hall in 1933. President Roosevelt set up the agency in that year under the National Industrial Recovery Act. It established codes of fair competition for business and industry but was later declared unconstitutional.

147. The hungry form a line at the 10¢ soup kitchen operated by Goodwill Industries at the Calvary Methodist Church. Reverend Theodore Grob and Methodist Deaconess Pauline Bartruff stand in the doorway. Contributions of Home Packing's pigs feet, bones, and brains; Quaker Maid's dented cans of vegetables; and Miller-Parrott's "day-old bread" make up the major portion of these meals, which were called "beans, bones and brains" by the workers.

148. Pork is distributed to those in need at the Light House Mission, 119 Ohio Street.

149. Members of a WPA Sewing Project at Torner Community House display their work in 1941. This community center, at 1107 S. 4th Street, was purchased with funds left by Rebecca Torner, a teacher who had taught German at Wiley High School for 35 years.

The Girls Club of Terre Haute, a charter member of the Girls Clubs of America, was established at the center in 1945.

National Headlines

Two local events received national coverage: the General Strike and the visit by Earl Browder.

The May 1939 issue of *Fortune* reported, "Terre Haute picks itself up from a general strike and solves a tense labor-capital tie-up with a superdose of boosterism," and told of the local Jaycees' success in these efforts. The magazine's view may have been more positive than that of many Terre Hauteans.

150. Earl Browder, U.S. Communist Party presidential candidate in 1936 and 1940, arrived in Terre Haute on September 30, 1936 and was arrested at Union Depot for vagrancy. Chief of Police Yates stated, "Anyone advertising himself as belonging to the Communist Party will not be permitted to speak in Terre Haute."

The next day, Indiana State Teachers College cancelled the contract for the hall where Browder was to speak, the charges against him were dismissed, and Browder was sent on his way. He later filed a damage suit against the mayor and the police chief.

151. One of the 22,658 strikes called in the nation during the 1930s was caused by a dispute between the Columbian Enameling and Stamping Co. and Federal Labor Union #19694. The "closed shop" became the major issue, and the workers began striking on March 23, 1935.

As tensions increased on both sides, the union, protesting the importation of out-of-town "strike breakers," called for a labor holiday. A general strike closed down business and transportation on July 22, 1935. National guardsmen moved into the county, as Governor Paul V. McNutt, acting on a request from the mayor, ordered martial law. Tear gas was used to disperse the pickets. The two-day general strike was called off, but the strike at the mill continued and martial law was in effect for six months.

This was the third general strike in the history of the United States. The first, in Seattle in 1919, lasted five days; and the second, in San Francisco in 1934, was in effect for three days.

World War II

World War II began with Germany's invasion of Poland in 1939. After the December 7, 1941 attack on Pearl Harbor, the United States declared war on Japan, and a few days later found itself at war with Germany and Italy. Before the fighting was over, 211 Vigo County military personnel were killed or missing in action.

Germany surrendered on May 7, 1945, and Japan opened peace negotiations on August 10, 1945, one day after an atomic bomb fell on Nagasaki.

152. "We're buying at least 10%" was the slogan portrayed in this 1942 photograph. Employees of the Vigo Ordinance, located south of the city, where the Pfizer Co. now stands, were recognized for their purchase of bonds.

153. The Big Four Depot was the point of departure in April 1941 for these 182 men chosen by Vigo County's four selective service boards working under the first peacetime draft in U.S. history. A parade and a patriotic program were held in their honor.

154. Salvation Army women serve doughnuts at the Terre Haute House to promote the sale of war bonds in 1945. The organization has been active locally since 1888.

155. Servicemen found a warm welcome and relaxation in this stone cottage at N. 6th and Cherry streets. This photograph is dated April 1943.

156. Members of the Women's Army Auxiliary Corps (WAACS) line up at the Terre Haute House in preparation for the 1943 Armistice Day observance.

157. Air raid wardens, Post 1, Sector 40, of the Office of Civil Defense, were photographed on May 13, 1943.

158. Members of the Krietenstein Post No. 104, American Legion, and members of the Navy V-12 color guard join in a ceremony on the Indiana State Teachers College campus, August 9, 1943.

159. These local National Youth Administration workers train for jobs in industry in 1943, the year the agency was terminated. Created in 1935, it provided an employment and work-relief program for persons aged 16–25 years. First a part of WPA, it became a part of the Federal Security Agency and then of the War Manpower Commission.

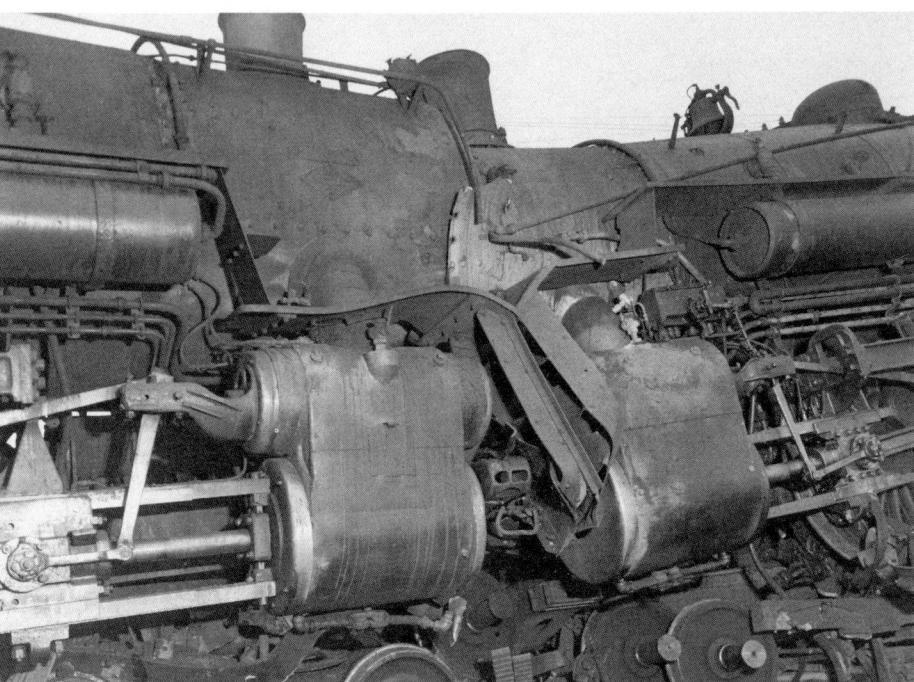

161. The night of September 14, 1944, these two locomotives crashed head-on at Dewey, near N. 25th Street and Haythorne Avenue on the C. & E. I. Railroad. Three crewmen and 26 servicemen en route from Chicago to Miami for rest and relaxation after overseas duty were killed. Ten railroad employees and 32 passengers were injured.

160. On this snowy January day in 1943, members of Ft. Harrison Post No. 40, American Legion, cut the Steeg Park cannon from its moorings and transported it to the scrap heap as part of the war effort.

162. The Miller-Parrott Baking Co. received the Army-Navy E pennant in 1943 for giving the highest degree of production in the war effort.

The company had a long local history, beginning with the Miller Bros. Bakery in 1880. Before Pearl Harbor, Victor Miller, president, worked with Army researchers to perfect an emergency ration biscuit.

163. Grocers were required to collect ration points as well as cash during the war period. Pictured here is Ernest L. Zwerner in his store at 1244 Lafayette Avenue. Glass milk bottles, not cartons or plastic containers, were in use.

164. Smokers line up at Hooks Drugs to buy a pack of cigarettes during the 1945 shortage. This photograph was included in a special issue of the *Tribune-Star* Rotogravure designed to be mailed to local servicemen and women stationed around the world.

165. A vegetable garden was not just a garden during the war; it was a "Victory Garden." Mrs. McCourt is pictured here tending her 1943 crop of vegetables.

A Certain Notoriety

"How's Sin in Terre Haute? Oh, About Like Anyplace"

were the words heading John Ackelmire's column in the Indianapolis *News* shortly after a February 1961 issue of the *Saturday Evening Post* featured Terre Haute as the "most notorious vice spot in Indiana." Needless to say, the "sin city" appellation came from a mixture of urban rivalry, sensationalist journalism, and fact. No place holds a monopoly on virtue.

A sampling is presented here.

Corruption

Impeachment proceedings were brought against Mayor Frank Bidaman in 1906. Charges included (1) non-enforcement of laws against prostitution and of laws regarding the closing of saloons, and (2) ignoring the publicity ordinance, which gave police authority to forcibly enter a room if they suspected that gambling was going on inside. The impeachment act failed by one vote in January but succeeded in June. Bidaman was replaced in office by Frank Buckingham.

166. Donn M. Roberts, a local contractor, was elected mayor of Terre Haute in 1913. While in office, he was convicted of federal election fraud, for which he served three-and-one-half years in federal prison. Roberts began the operation of local gasoline stations in 1929 and was convicted of gasoline tax embezzlement in 1936. He suffered a heart attack in prison and died one month after his conviction.

Gambling

The amount of local gambling activity changed as governmental administrations played "political football" with the issue. Local headlines with the same meaning as those printed below appeared off and on through the first 50 years of this century.

September 30, 1918   LID GOES OFF, GAMBLING NOW IN FULL BLAST
November 9, 1920   GAMBLERS ALLEGED CROOKED BY LOSER
March 25, 1941   SHERIFF APPLIES LID ON GAMBLING
February 22, 1943   GAMBLING RAIDS BRING ARRESTS
December 13, 1948   SEIZE 47 SLOT MACHINES HERE

—from the Terre Haute *Tribune*

Prostitution

Terre Haute's "Red Light District" was located in the area bordered by Water, N. 4th, Cherry, and Chestnut streets. It has been said it once contained as many as 50 houses and 250 to 300 women.

    The district developed during the Civil War and remained until World War II. Mayor Vernon McMillan closed down the houses, forcing the madams to move beyond the city limits. After the war prostitution began again, but on a smaller scale. The properties were acquired by the city's Department of Redevelopment and torn down during the 1960s.

167. and 168. The most famous house was that of Madam Edith Brown, at 206 N. Second Street, pictured here in 1941. She opened her first house in 1901 at 213 Mulberry Street and was located from 1906 to 1916 at 318 Eagle Street.

Family and Neighborhood Life

169, 170, 171, 172, and 173. "Home is where the heart is" is translated by city and country dwellers alike into "Home is where the Wabash Valley is." Max Ehrmann's short statement expresses it best of all: "Here is the world in miniature."

174. Nostalgia surrounds the Irishman's Covered Bridge, built in 1845 over Honey Creek in Riley Township. It was moved to Fowler Park in 1971 with funds raised by the Girl Scouts, the Vigo County Historical Society, area residents, and employees of the Columbian Enameling & Stamping Co.

175. This couple is busy making soap at their farm in northwestern Vigo County. The date is unknown.

176. Darwin Ferry, connecting Vigo County and Clark County, Illinois, is shown in the rural setting of Prairie Creek Township. At the time of this photograph, 1949, three passenger cars could be transported across the river in three to four minutes for 35¢ per car.

177. A peddler brings his merchandise to the people of Prairieton Township.

178. Francis Marion Kibler and two unidentified boys pose in front of Kibler's Feed Mill about 1900. Note the U.S. Army recruiting sign on the right.
   The Kibler business remains in operation on Paris Avenue in West Terre Haute.

179. A horse and buggy wait patiently while the men and boys pose in front of this Prairieton General Store. The Model Ice Cream sign indicates that the photograph was taken in 1911 or later, since the company was formed in that year.

180. and 181. Good neighbors are indispensable! In December 1948 the Jolly Pals, an organization of the Farmers Chapel Church, harvest the crop belonging to Arthur Morris, who has a fractured hip. The farm is on County Line Road between Prairie Creek and Farmersburg.

Good cooks are busy in the kitchen. The Clermont cook stove holds an abundance of food to be served when the men return from the fields.

182. The city of Terre Haute is surrounded by a number of picturesque, old mining towns out in the rural areas. One of these is Fontanet in Nevins Township. The early settlers named their settlement "Fountain" for a fountainhead or spring that flowed to a point where the town is located. The name was changed to "Fontanett," because another Indiana post office was using the name "Fountain." Eventually "Fontanett" became "Fontanet."

183. The DuPont Powder Mill, which made blasting powder for use in neighboring coal mines, exploded in 1907 causing 27 deaths, scores of serious burns and injuries, and extensive damage in the Fontanet area. The Billy Judson home is pictured here following the disaster.

184. It appears to be a slow day for business in Prairie Creek in the 1920s.

185. Hurshel Hill's North Terre Haute Feed Store was located on the south side of Park Avenue near the Otter Creek Township School. It is five minutes before noon on this 1944 day, according to the Vitality clock. The temperature on the Mail Pouch Tobacco thermometer is not visible.

186. Persons and property outside the city limits are protected by neighbors organized into township volunteer fire departments. The Otter Creek Volunteer Fire Department was founded in 1943, following a fire that destroyed three businesses, killed one man, and threatened to damage all of North Terre Haute.

The first firehouse was located on land given by the Knights of Pythias; the present facility was built on land donated by Dr. Don Gerrish.

187. North 7th Street Road was "country" back in 1904. The J. J. Martin residence is in the foreground, and the Frank J. Martin home can be seen in the distance. The latter was torn down in the 1960s to make space for U.S. 41.

188. Neighborhood communication decreased when front porches disappeared. The porch was a place to sit, to visit, to court, and, of course, to pose for a photograph. This is the Moses Myers home at 317 N. 9th Street just before 1900.

189. A neighborhood on the banks of the Wabash River is pictured at flood stage early in our century.

190. The Preston House, the oldest residence still in existence in Terre Haute, was constructed at 13½ and Poplar streets between 1823 and 1827 by Major George W. Dewees, a wealthy New Orleans businessman. It became the property of Nathaniel Preston in 1843.

192. Members of the John McFall's sleigh party enjoy a snowy day in February 1934.

191. A favorite spot for winter sledding was and still is Strawberry Hill on Seabury Avenue coming down from S. Sixth Street. The photograph is dated December 30, 1943.

Neighborhood Grocery Stores

The neighborhood store was much more than a place to buy food and household supplies. It was also a place to meet neighbors and catch up on the latest happenings.

A total of 433 retail grocery stores are listed in the 1925 *City Directory*.

193. Live chickens and a neat display of produce are part of the promotion at this Oakley Store, 1101 Wabash Avenue, some time between 1928 and 1930. The chain of Oakley's Economy Stores included 36 stores in the city, two in West Terre Haute, and one in North Terre Haute. In 1929 the general office was located at 200 N. 10½ Street.

195. Bread is 9¢ a loaf and Quaker Oats 8¢ a package on this October day in 1925. The Great Atlantic & Pacific Tea Company operated fourteen stores in Terre Haute at that time.

194. Edward, Jr., and Walter Paitson opened their grocery at 1474 Locust Street in 1919. They specialized in freshly baked goods and meat. Their brother Fred was the baker in the early 1920s, the period when this photograph was taken. The store continued in business until 1979.

Two other Paitson brothers, Stanley and Robert, had a service station behind the grocery and sold hardware from the station. Later they formed the Paitson Bros. Hardware Company, which remains in business on Wabash Avenue.

196. Twelve Points, the northside business community pictured here in 1950, has been the location of banks, restaurants, saloons, groceries, and drug and variety stores since the turn of the century. In 1890 Walter Phillips built his home at Lafayette and Grand Avenues. Seven years later he began to purchase land and build business buildings at the intersection of Maple and Lafayette avenues and N. 13th Street. Phillips died in 1939.

197. "May we help you?" ask the clerks at the William J. Danner Dry Goods Store, 1260-64 Lafayette Avenue, in 1925. Other Twelve Points dry goods stores in business that year were John H. Swander, 2068 N. 13th Street, and Twelve Points Dry Goods Co., 1238 Lafayette Avenue.

198. C. B. and Lettie May Thomas founded the Thomas Funeral Home in Rosedale in 1907. Ten years later they moved to the Harley James Livery Stable in Twelve Points. The first motorized funeral vehicle, a Studebaker, was purchased in 1920. The present building is shown in 1925, three years after its construction.

199. Easter Week, 1913, is a memorable time in local history. It began with a tornado striking Terre Haute on Easter Sunday, March 23. The floods that followed the storm devastated Sugar Creek Township as well as parts of Terre Haute.

200. and 201. On the evening of May 21, 1949, a tornado struck the eastern edge of Terre Haute, killing two men at Deming Park. These pictures, taken at Hulman Field, show the storm over Deming Park and the destruction at the Nattkemper home at Fruitridge and Wallace avenues.

202. This 1913 flood scene shows Taylorville, across the Wabash River to the west, under water.

203. 204. 205. Scenes in West Terre Haute.

The 1943 Flood

May 10 River up, flood warnings issued.
May 17 River at 21.4 ft.
May 18 Troops on duty; West Terre Haute and Dresser families evacuated.
May 19 River at all-time high. Chicago, Milwaukee, St. Paul & Pacific Railroad bridge washed out; 27,000 acres of farm land flooded.
May 20 Crews sandbagging.
May 21 River crests at 30.5 ft.
May 22 Waters begin to recede.

Medicine

The beginning of the Vigo County Medical Society dates back to the founding of the Aesculapian Society of the Wabash Valley in 1846. The local group became the oldest continuous medical society west of the Alleghenies.

The Society, the Rose Dispensary, and St. Anthony's and Union hospitals are all prominent in local medical history.

206. The Terre Haute Sanitarium was founded in 1892 by Dr. B. F. Swafford and Dr. L. J. Weinstein in a small frame house on N. 7th Street. A group representing various church denominations took over the hospital in 1895, and the name was changed to Union Home for Invalids of Terre Haute. Construction of the seven story brick building at N. 7th Street and 8th Avenue began in 1922. It became Union Hospital, Inc. in 1935.

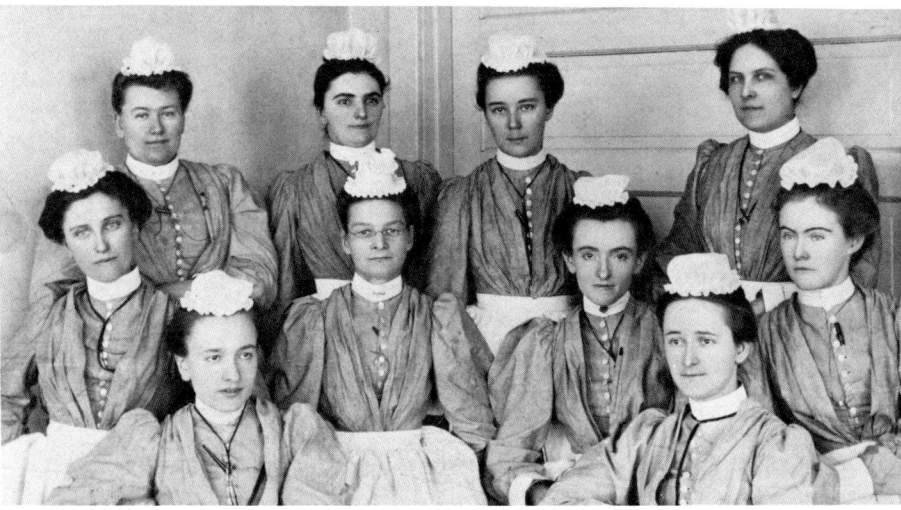

207. The Training School for Nurses opened in 1900 and continued as the Union Hospital School of Nursing until 1965. An early graduating class is pictured here.

208. The Rose Dispensary Building, pictured here in 1935, was a downtown landmark at N. 7th and Cherry streets. Constructed in 1894–1895, it housed the Rose Dispensary, which served medical indigents for more than 70 years. It provided free dental care, eye care, medical attention, and medication with funds left in trust for this purpose by Chauncey Rose.

The building was sold in 1970 to Indiana State University and was razed in 1972 to make room for a parking lot.

209. St. Anthony's Hospital, founded in 1882, was first located at 2nd and Mulberry streets. When it opened it was the only hospital in the city, for Providence Hospital, founded by Chauncey Rose, had been closed for several years.

The building, purchased for the Poor Sisters of St. Francis by Mr. and Mrs. Herman Hulman, Sr., soon proved inadequate. St. Agnes Hall for girls became available and was purchased for the hospital by Mr. Hulman.

The institution opened at the new S. 6th Street location in 1884. It was acquired by the Hospital Corporation of America in 1975, but the building was closed in 1979 when the Terre Haute Regional Hospital on S. 7th Street was completed. All the St. Anthony buildings were demolished in 1982.

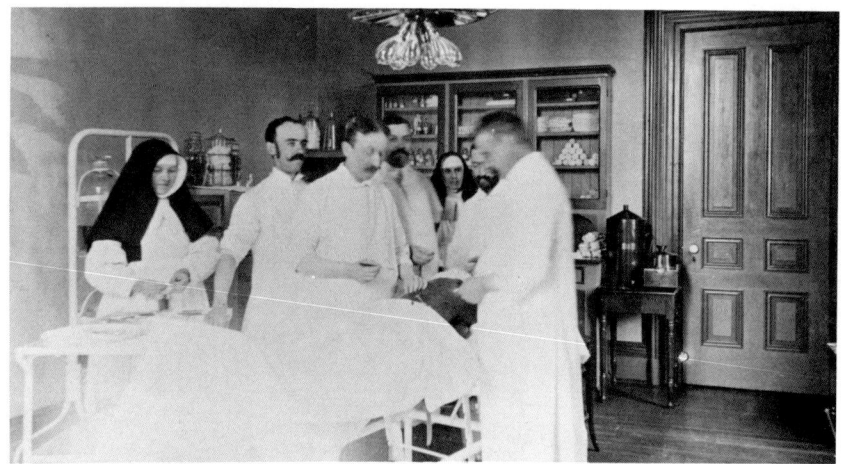

210. Surgery at the hospital at the turn of the century is pictured here.

Education

211. The first subscription school in the county was established in 1817. The voters decided in favor of free schools in 1848, but it took several years for free, public education to be offered. The county became an educational center with the founding of St. Mary's Female Institute, Indiana State Normal School, and Rose Polytechnic Institute.

St. Mary-of-the-Woods College

St. Mary's Female Institute was founded in 1841 by Mother Theodore Guerin and five Sisters of Providence from France. Classes were offered to girls on the wooded campus in northwestern Vigo County now known as St. Mary-of-the-Woods College. The first charter for the higher education of women in Indiana was granted in 1846; the first bachelor of arts degree was conferred in 1899. The school is now recognized as the oldest Catholic liberal arts college for women in the U.S.

212. The Church of the Immaculate Conception, a resource of the Sisters of Providence, was consecrated in 1907.

213. The month of May has a special history at the Woods. A queen and her court are shown in 1935; the last May Day ceremony was held in 1968.

214. The cornerstone of the first building was laid in 1875, and the institute formally opened in 1883. In 1922 the campus was moved from its original site at N. 13th and Locust streets to its present location on the eastern edge of the city, and the old building became Gerstmeyer High School.

215. 1918

216. 1941

Rose Polytechnic Institute

Chauncey Rose provided funds for the founding of "an institute for the intellectual and practical education of young men" in 1874. Rose Polytechnic Institute was the first private engineering college west of the Allegheny Mountains. Renamed Rose-Hulman Institute of Technology in 1971, the college has a national reputation for excellence in science and engineering education.

217. An ROTC review is part of the day's activity in front of the main classroom building, now Moench Hall, on October 11, 1949.

218. The Normal Training School was built in 1905 on the campus facing south on Mulberry Street. Classes were moved to the new Laboratory School, N. 7th and Chestnut streets, in 1935.

219. The cornerstone of the first campus building was laid in 1867. The doors were opened to 21 students in January 1870. The building was destroyed by fire in 1888.

220. The second administration building was constructed in 1889. Enrollment in the early 1900s was 400–500; by 1947 it had increased to 2,555.

Indiana State Teachers College

Indiana State Teachers College, created by an act of the Indiana General Assembly in 1865, is Indiana's second oldest state university. The City of Terre Haute offered $50,000 plus land located near the center of the city and valued at $25,000 to the State Normal School Board to acquire the site for Terre Haute. Through the years the campus has expanded in size, the courses of study have been broadened, and the name has been changed: Indiana State Normal School (1870–1929), Indiana State Teachers College (1929–1961), Indiana State College (1961–1965), and Indiana State University (since 1965).

221. The second administration building is in the process of being demolished in April 1950. The present administration building appears to the left.

222. Trees shade the entrance of "Old Main" in May 1938.

223. A float in the 1945 Homecoming Parade approaches the intersection of 7th Street and Wabash Avenue. The first Homecoming event was held in 1913, and the first Homecoming Parade marched in 1923. Today the annual parade is the largest of its kind in the nation.

224. Students were changing classes in this 1948 campus scene photographed from the top of Central Christian Church.

225. and 226. The Terre Haute Library Association established a public library in 1882. In 1903 Crawford Fairbanks gave $50,000 for a new library in memory of his mother. The Emeline Fairbanks Memorial Library opened in 1906 at 222 N. 7th Street. The reading room is pictured here in 1930.

Library services were extended to all of Vigo County in 1961. A new Vigo County Public Library building was constructed at S. 7th and Walnut streets in 1979, and the Fairbanks Library closed its doors. The building now belongs to Indiana State University.

227. Students in a touch-typing class at the Terre Haute Commercial College (third floor, 25 S. 7th Street) are hard at work in this 1934 photograph. Garvin, Wabash, Brown, and Wabash-Brown were other names associated with local business schools. Miss Kelley's Private Shorthand School offered instruction in 1915–16.

Wiley High School

228. The Terre Haute High School opened in 1886 at S. 7th and Walnut streets. The name was changed in 1906 to Wiley High School to honor W. H. Wiley, city school superintendent. The building remained the home of the Wiley Red Streaks until 1971, the year in which the new Terre Haute South and North Vigo high schools were opened. The old high school building was demolished and the Vigo County Public Library has replaced it. The cupola that decorated the school building for 85 years is now part of the library grounds.

229. A track meet is one of the events of the Wiley GAA (Girls' Athletic Association) play day in 1950.

Garfield High School

230. Garfield High School opened in 1912. Its Maple Avenue location filled a longtime need of northside residents. The school was named after President James A. Garfield, a strong supporter of public education.

The main building was gutted by fire in 1934, and classes were held in Twelve Points buildings until repairs could be made. WPA workers furnished the labor for the gymnasium, which was completed in 1938.

The home of the Purple Eagles was closed at the end of the school year in 1971, and the building was razed in 1973. It is now the site of Garfield Gardens and Tower Apartments.

231. This Garfield pep session is part of the 1948–49 school year.

Gerstmeyer Technical High School

232. The Gerstmeyer building at N. 13th and Locust streets was formerly occupied by Rose Polytechnic Institute. The boys from the vocational school (Lafayette and 3rd avenues) were moved into the vacated building in 1922 and were joined three years later by the students from the girls' vocational school (S. 6½ and Poplar streets). The school was named in honor of Dr. Charles Gerstmeyer, a local physician and school board member who contributed funds to help establish a vocational department in the city schools. The doors closed on the Tech Black Cats in 1971, and the original building was demolished. Chauncey Rose Junior High School now occupies the site.

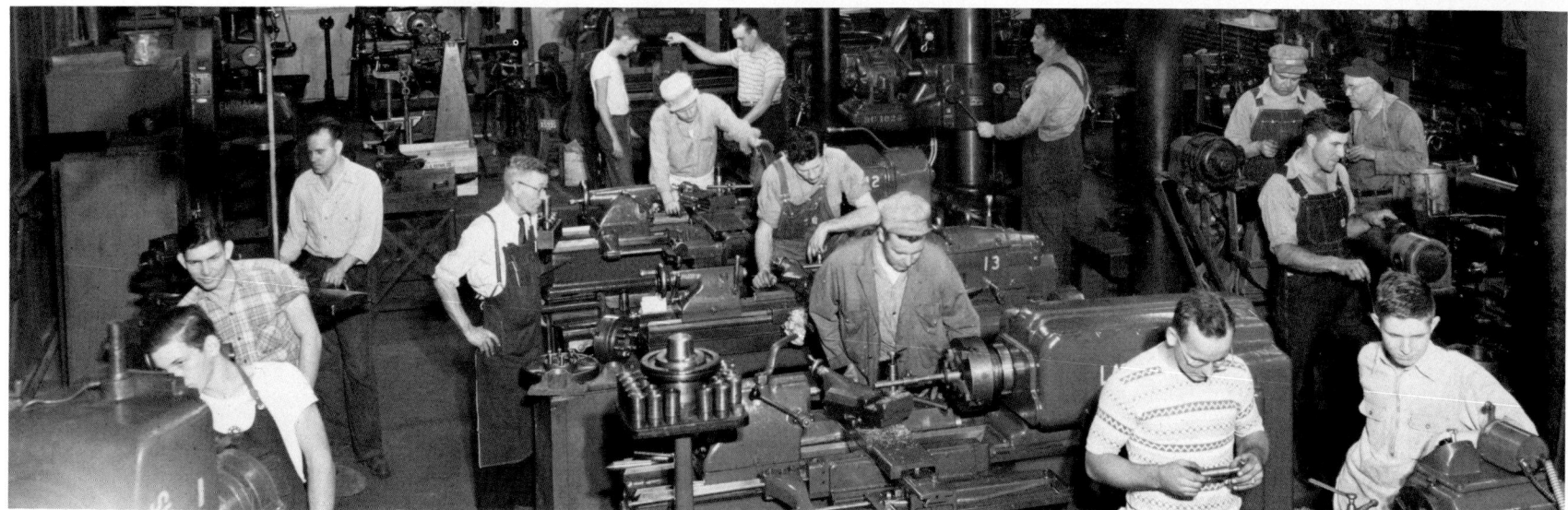

233. An adult education class at the school in 1949.

234. The 1925 Eighth Grade Graduating Class at Fort Harrison School appears here. Harry G. Huntwork was the principal. The building, located at the corner of N. 8th Street and Ft. Harrison Road, has been occupied by several church organizations since it was sold in 1962.

235. The horse-drawn school hack was the forerunner of the school bus. These hacks and several like them carried Pierson Township students to Blackhawk School. Students sat facing each other on benches along each side of the interior of the wagon. A coal oil (kerosene) heater supplied warmth in cold weather.

On arrival the horses were unhitched and housed in stables at the school until time to take the students home. The drivers shown are Otto Miller and James Pierson.

236. Until 1960, when the citizens of Vigo County voted to consolidate all school u into the Vigo County School Corporation, students outside the city districts attende township schools. This school in Lost Creek Township was located six miles east of city on U.S. 40, in the Glenn area.

237. A flower show was held at the Booker T. Washington School, 1101 S. 13th Street, in August 1949.

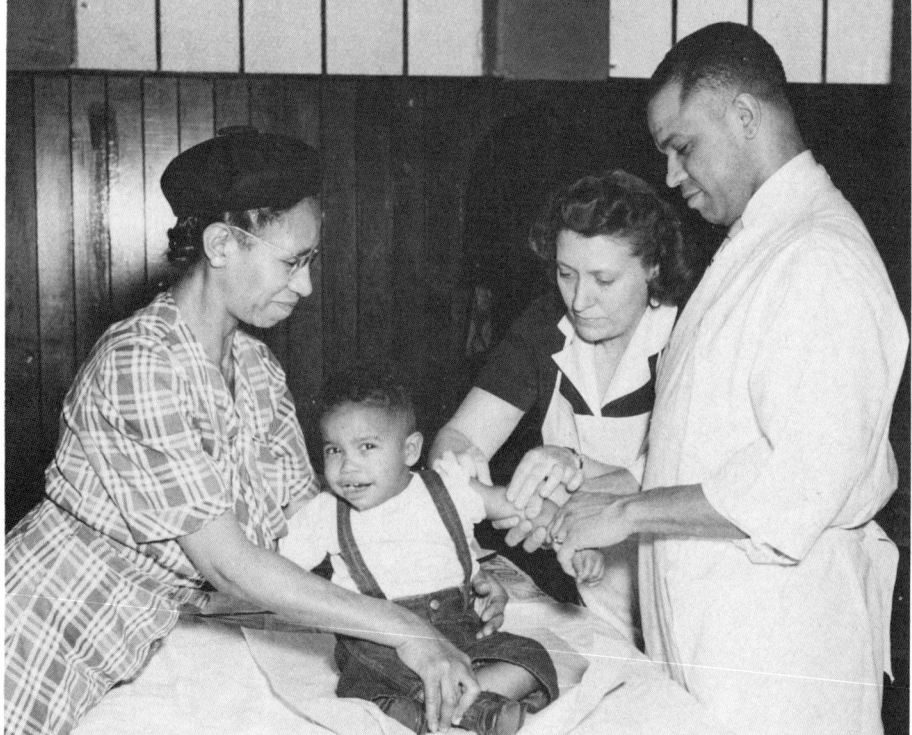

238. This young man is the smiling subject of examination at the Well Child Clinic sponsored by the Highland School P.T.A. in 1949. Highland School was located at the northeast corner of Elizabeth Avenue and N. 15th Street.

239. Black youngsters in a Terre Haute classroom figured in a series of school photographs prepared by Superintendent William H. Wiley for an exhibit at the 1904 Chicago World's Fair. After the state desegregation law was passed in 1949, black students could choose between the elementary school in their neighborhood and the "for colored only" school that they had been attending.

240. The King Classical School, a private day school founded by Bertha Pratt King and Mary Sinclair Crawford in 1906, offered classes to Terre Haute youngsters until 1945. The school soon outgrew its original home at 681 Oak Street, and in two years it moved to the southwest corner of S. 6th and Park streets, where it was located until its closing.

241. Constructed with WPA labor, the Dresser Elementary School opened its doors in 1936 to 300 students in eight grades with seven teachers. The new school was an improvement over the Taylorville School which it replaced. Records indicate that the same number of students were served by only three teachers in the old building in 1916.

In 1971 the classes were transferred to West Vigo Elementary School. The Kerman Grotto now occupies the site.

242. The Gibault Home for Boys was dedicated in 1921 at the former Fred B. Smith estate on the west side of U.S. 41 south of the city. Sponsored by the Indiana Knights of Columbus, the home provides a "refuge for wayward boys." In 1934 the administration of the school was assumed by the Brothers of Holy Cross from Notre Dame at the invitation of the Indiana Knights of Columbus. Enrollment grew to more than 100 boys within a few years. The original house has been demolished but the school remains on the property.

Cultural Activities

Leigh Hunt, a nineteenth-century English poet, wrote "There are two worlds: the world that we can measure with line and rule, and the world that we feel with our hearts and imaginations." This second world is reflected in the cultural side of the community. Through the years art, music, drama, literature, and history have found a significant place in Terre Haute life.

243. Fourteen local citizens met in 1922 to discuss the possibility of organizing a local historical society. In 1923 the Vigo County Historical Society was formally founded. Members are pictured on the steps of the Emeline Fairbanks Memorial Library, where the organization met until 1958. The Sage-Robinson-Nagel home, 1411 S. 6th Street, was donated in 1957, and the Society's Historical Museum of the Wabash Valley opened one year later.

244. Members of the Woman's Department Club unveil the Janet Scudder Memorial Fountain on their grounds in 1941. The club, the successor to the Local Council of Women's Clubs, was founded in 1920 and reached a membership of 1,087 by 1929. The present clubhouse, the former Hudson residence at 507 S. 6th Street, was purchased in 1931.

Miss Juliet Peddle, Mrs. Gilbert Gambill, Mrs. Glenn Andrew, Mrs. Malcolm Steele, Mrs. Walker Schell, Mrs. Jane Kimball Yung, and Mrs. E. T. Hazledine are pictured here.

245. Swope Art Gallery is the realization of the dream of Terre Haute merchant Sheldon Swope. He gave the Swope Block, at the northwest corner of S. 7th and Ohio streets, for the gallery's home and other properties to provide funds necessary to open and maintain the facility. The Gallery was formally opened on March 23, 1942; its collection and exhibits have achieved nationwide renown.

Among the local artists who were recognized nationally and sometimes internationally during the first half of this century were Janet Scudder and Caroline Peddle Ball, sculptors; Gilbert Wilson, painter and muralist; and Amelia Kussner Coudert, miniaturist.

246. Paul Dresser, 1858–1906, was the son of John Paul and Sarah Mary Dreiser and the older brother of Theodore Dreiser. He was one of the most successful songwriters of Tin Pan Alley in the 1890s, and his sentimental ballads stayed popular into the twentieth century.

His song "On the Banks of the Wabash, Far Away" became the State Song of Indiana by act of the state legislature in 1913. His Terre Haute birthplace, a pre–Civil War workingman's house, has been designated as a State Shrine and is listed in the National Register of Historic Places. It was moved from 318 S. Second Street to Fairbanks Park by the Vigo County Historical Society in 1963.

247. Theodore Dreiser, 1871–1945, was born in Terre Haute and baptized at St. Benedict Church. He lived in Vincennes, Sullivan, Evansville, and Warsaw before leaving Indiana at a young age. He became one of the most important American novelists of the twentieth century.

His writing, which dealt with the harsh realities of life and was tempered by compassion for the common man, contrasted sharply with the popular romanticism of his day. The controversial *Sister Carrie* (1900) was his first novel and *An American Tragedy* (1925) his best known work.

248. Max Ehrmann, 1872–1945, poet and philosopher, made Terre Haute his home. He wrote, "What place is lovelier than Terre Haute . . . many a forward-looking son has found the gifts the gods have here bestowed."

After graduating from DePauw University and studying at Harvard University, Ehrmann returned and pursued a career in business and law. By age 40, he devoted himself entirely to literature.

An idealist, Ehrmann wrote from a philosophy of love and hope with a deep feeling for the beauty and goodness in life. His "A Prayer" (1906) and "Desiderata" (1927) are internationally known.

249. A spectacular International Revue was a production of the Children's Theatre of Terre Haute in 1950. More than 300 children and college students took part, including Kay Maurice, Janice Felstein, Carol Smith, and Joy Vari, shown here making their entrance.

The Children's Theatre was founded in 1936 under the leadership of Mrs. Oscar Baur.

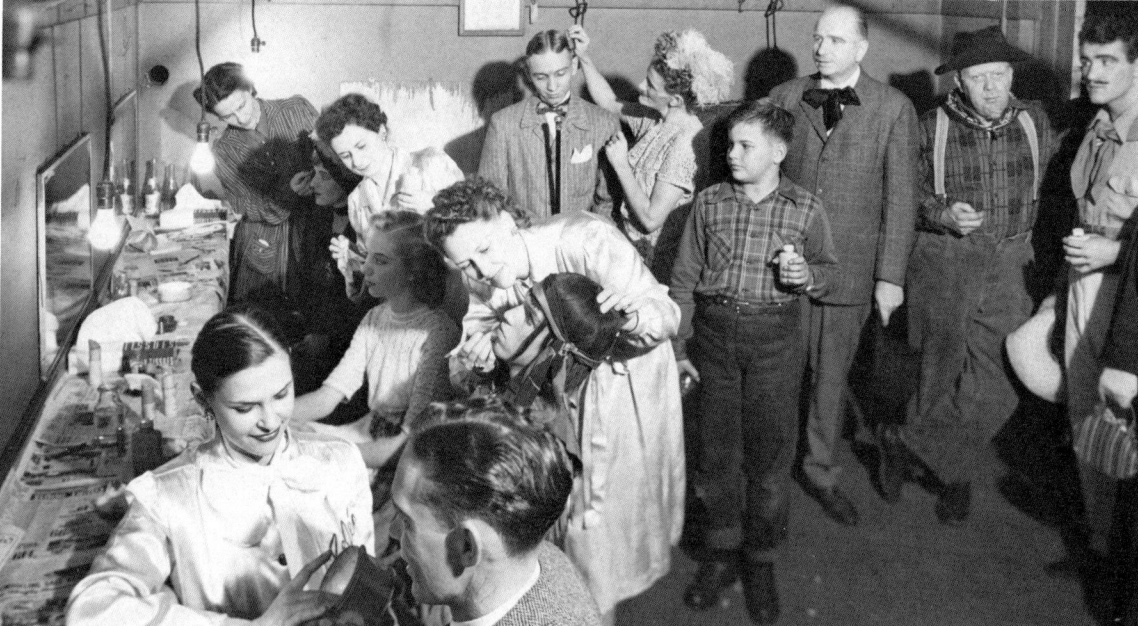

250. Make-up artists are busy behind the scenes of *Chicken Every Sunday,* produced by the Community Theatre of Terre Haute in 1947.

This local theatre group was organized by Madge Polk Townsley in 1926 and is the second oldest amateur theatre in Indiana. Plays were produced on a number of local stages before the Best Theatre, at S. 25th Street and Washington Avenue was purchased, remodeled, and opened as the Weldin Talley Memorial Playhouse.

251. Dr. Will Bryant, founder and first conductor of the Terre Haute Symphony, says good-bye to Terre Haute musicians before his departure for Greensboro, N. C., in 1949.

Bryant gathered 40 nonprofessional musicians to present the first concert on December 4, 1926, at the Indiana Theatre. This group came to be Indiana's second symphony orchestra. Dr. James Barnes began his 21-year tenure as conductor in 1949.

A Sense of Belonging

A multitude of past and present religious, service, and social groups have given inspiration and fellowship to community residents. Terre Haute has been called both a "city of churches" and a "city of joiners."

253. Allen Chapel, founded in 1837, moved into its present location at S. 3rd and Crawford streets in 1870. The structure was rebuilt after the 1913 tornado, which caused extensive fire damage.

Listed in the Register of Historic Places, Allen Chapel is the oldest black church in the city. This is an early view of the interior.

252. The Methodist Temple, at S. 7th and Poplar streets, pictured here in 1949, was built in 1895. It was vacated in 1969, when the congregation occupied its new church at 5001 Dixie Bee Road. The building was razed, and the site is now part of the Vigo County Public Library building and grounds.

The name "Methodist Temple" was adopted in the 1920s during an unsuccessful attempt to unite the congregations of the First Methodist and Centenary churches.

254. The First Baptist Church of Terre Haute was organized in 1837. In 1916 the congregation dedicated this building, pictured in 1931, at S. 6th and Walnut streets. After the congregation moved to its present church east of the city on Poplar Street in 1968, the old building was razed to provide additional parking space at the Associated Physicians & Surgeons Clinic.

255. Mayor Samuel Beecher greets His Eminence, Metropolitan Archbishop Anthony Bashir, in front of the church at 635 N. 5th Street during the late 1930s. Looking on were Joseph Malooley, Ossad Saikley, Nicholas Corey, City Clerk Jim Yates, and Reverend John Koury.

A Syrian community was established in Terre Haute by 1910. The former Voorhees School was purchased and remodeled for the church in 1927. The present church at 1900 S. 4th Street was constructed in 1957.

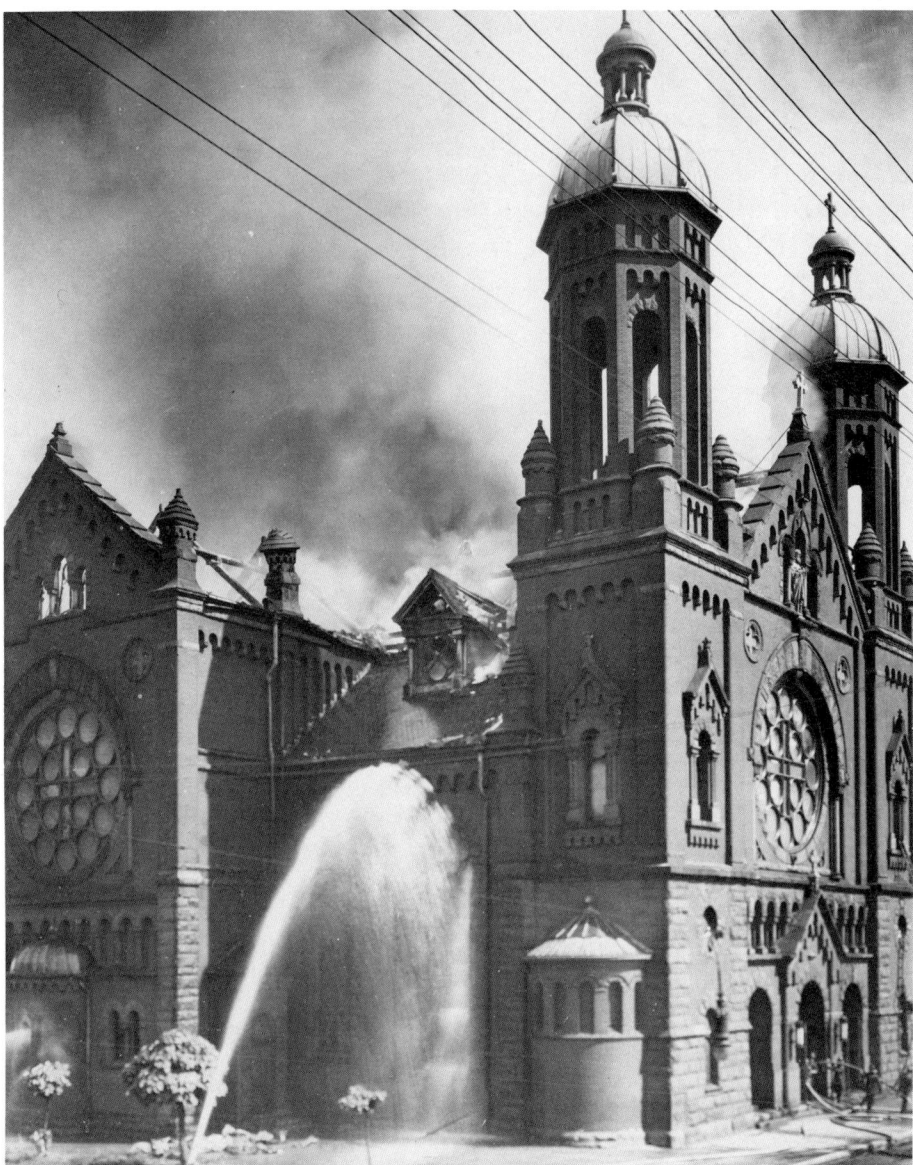

257. Fire destroys the dome and interior of St. Benedict Church on July 30, 1930. More than 6,000 people gathered to watch the spectacle.

This church, the second building of the parish, was dedicated in 1899. A German Catholic School was part of the parish organization from 1865, when the first church was constructed, until 1970.

256. These members of the clergy celebrate the 100th anniversary of St. Joseph Church in 1938. St. Joseph's was the first Roman Catholic church in Terre Haute. Construction began in 1837, and services were first held there in 1838.

258. From the beginning, individuals from other parts of the country and the world have come to the Wabash Valley to make their homes. The Roumanian community began to gather in the area of 25th Street and 4th Avenue about 1904. Their fraternal society hall at 1313 N. 25th Street was purchased and remodeled for St. Andrew Roumanian Orthodox Church in 1918.

259. Members of the Hungarian community lived in the area bounded by N. 19th and N. 24th streets and by Maple Avenue and Ash Street. Hungarian Hall was constructed in 1922 on the southeast corner of 22nd and Linden Streets. Until that time the lot was the First Terre Haute Hungarian Society Park and was surrounded by a high wooden fence. A tent and a portable dance floor were set up for special events.

260. Members of this 1945 class at Temple Israel are part of the United Hebrew Congregation, formed by the merger of Temple Israel and Temple B'nai Abraham in 1935. The latter group left their temple at Fifth and Poplar streets, which now houses the Wabash Senior Citizens center. The present Temple Israel building, at 540 S. 6th Street, was completed in 1911.

Jewish settlers made the Wabash Valley their home as early as the 1820s. The present congregation was the first completely integrated synagogue of Orthodox, Conservative, and Reform Jews in the country.

261. Glenn Home, 6500 Wabash Avenue, was an impressive sight in 1933. In 1901 the Vigo County Commissioners bought the Klatte farm as a site for a home for dependent children. The first youngsters arrived in July 1903. The County Welfare Department closed the facility in 1979, and the property was sold in 1980.

262. Residents of the Clara Fairbanks Home for Aged Women, 721 8th Avenue, tended to their knitting in December 1942. The cornerstone of the Home, a memorial from Crawford Fairbanks to his wife, was put in place in 1924.

The "Old Ladies Home" was formerly located at 6 Home Avenue and was conducted by WORD (Women's Organization of Retail Druggists) for several years. Another "Home for Aged Ladies" was operated by the Rose Ladies Aid Society at 1016 N. 6th Street. It was later called the Rose Aid Home.

263. Highland Lawn Cemetery, established on the site of the Jenckes farm east of the city in the 1880s, is more than a final resting place for Terre Hauteans. The beauty of the grounds make the cemetery a place to enjoy on a Sunday afternoon drive and a landmark to show off to out-of-town visitors.

264. A home for children from 1884 to 1950, Chauncey Rose School (Rose Orphans Home until 1930) was founded with funds provided by Chauncey Rose. The buildings at N. 25th Street and Wabash Avenue were demolished in 1966, and a K-Mart shopping center is now on the site.

265. The local Knights of Columbus organization was founded in 1900 in the Tune Building at 5th Street and Wabash Avenue. In 1905 it bought Thomas Kinser's red brick residence at 828 Ohio Street, which was used until 1971. After the purchase and remodeling of the former Standard Food Market at S. 9th and Poplar streets, the old Ohio Street home was razed in 1972.

266. The cornerstone for the Riley Masonic Lodge building was laid in October 1950.
Terre Haute Lodge 19, Free and Accepted Masons, established in 1819, was the first masonic lodge in the county. At the turn of the century Masons met at 644½ Wabash Avenue. Ground was broken for the present Terre Haute Masonic Temple, at 224 N. 8th Street, in 1915.

267. In the early 1900s the Benevolent and Protective Order of the Elks No. 86 met every Wednesday evening in Rooms 500–501 in the Opera House Block. Plans were made for their own building, and the laying of the cornerstone in 1908 is pictured here. The dedication speaker said, "There is nothing equal to it in the whole United States." The Elks sold this building to Indiana State University in 1970, when their new facilities at the Ft. Harrison Country Club were completed.

268. The Terre Haute YWCA, one of the earliest in Indiana, was organized in 1902. Its first home was the Samuel F. Early residence at 664 Ohio Street, and the second was the Universalist Church building at 119 N. 8th Street.

It was a proud day for the YWCA women when their own building, shown here, was completed in 1908. This facility, at 121 N. 7th Street, served thousands of Wabash Valley women and girls into the 1970s. The organization constructed a new home near Fairbanks Park, and this building was demolished in 1980.

269. Under the slogan "Trying to Make Men's Lives and Homes Better," a 1907 YMCA brochure offered an exercise class, bowling alleys, instruction in mechanical drawing, English for foreigners, a billiard and pool room, Saturday Night "Pop," and a Bible class at the building pictured here at 644 Ohio Street.

The Young Men's Christian Association moved to this location from the northeast corner of S. 7th and Ohio streets in 1903 and remained there until the present building at S. 6th and Walnut streets was opened in 1940.

270. Goodwill Industries was founded locally in 1927 by Reverend Theodore Grob. The first Goodwill building was located in the parsonage of his church (Calvary Methodist) at 126 N. 5th Street.

271. The Wabash Valley Council of Boy Scouts was organized in 1912 with Walter Haley as the first president. In this 1930 photograph, the Drum and Bugle Corps is lined up in front of the headquarters in Heminway Park, at the corner of 7th and Chestnut streets. It is now part of the grounds of the Indiana State University Laboratory School. Later the office was moved from 1235 Ohio Street to its present building at 501 S. 25th Street. This property, dedicated in 1959, and the house in Heminway Park were the gifts of the Hollie and Anna Oakley family.

272. The first local Girl Scout Troop was organized in 1918 at the YWCA. Pauline Bartruff and Mrs. H. L. McGurk were two of the early leaders. By 1940 there were 38 active troops. In this 1945 photograph, Brownie Scouts are departing from the Little House headquarters, 530 N. Center Street, for an annual outing at McCormick's Creek State Park.

The Council moved from the Little House in 1962 to 229½ S. 5th Street and then to 710 Seabury Street, before building its new headquarters adjacent to Fairbanks Park in 1973.

Community Fund Agencies, 1930

Child Welfare Association
Colored Day Nursery
Flora Gulick Boys Club
Florence Crittenden Home
Fresh Air Mission
Light House Mission
Phyllis Wheatley Association
Public Health Nursing Association
Rose Old Ladies Home
Society for Organizing Charity
Terre Haute Chapter, American Red Cross
Volunteers of America

274. The Light House Mission has served the needs of transient and local persons since the 1890s, when it was established under the sponsorship of the First Congregational Church. The 119–125 Ohio Street building pictured here in 1926 was dedicated in 1908 and used until the mission moved to its present site at N. 12th and Eagle streets.

273. This giant red feather draws attention to the Community Chest campaign in 1948. It was attached to the headquarters of the CIO council Benefit Association, 671 Wabash Avenue.

275. Ted Moore, director of the Terre Haute Boys Club from 1939 to 1971, shares a bit of nature study with the members at Camp Gulick in 1945. From left to right are Lex Nichols, George House, and Moore. The camp property in Parke County was the gift of C. J. Root in 1940. Flora Gilman Gulick founded the club in 1908 in the Social Settlement kitchen at First and Cherry streets. As membership grew, the club moved three times before it was located at 220 N. 3rd Street. With the help of the Lions Club, the gym was added in 1927 and the present building was completed in 1951.

Leisure Time

Spare time and holidays were spent in a variety of sports, recreation, and entertainment activities.

276. Collett Park, the oldest park in the city, is the scene of this 1922 tennis match. Josephus Collett gave his wood pasture between 7th and 9th streets, north of Maple Avenue, to the city in 1888 for use as a park. He also provided $2,500 for a streetcar line to serve the area.

277. These young women are enjoying a lovely summer day at Forest Park, located on 365 acres north of the city. A two-mile boating course on Otter Creek, bathing and fishing in an artificial lake, a dancing pavilion, and refreshments and meals served by Miles McNeal could be a part of a day at the park in 1915. Jitney service to and from the park was available at all hours.

278. Swimmers enjoy the pool at Fairbanks Park in June 1938. The pool was demolished after it had not been used for more than twenty years.

279. This peaceful summer scene in Fairbanks Park on July 16, 1945 is in sharp contrast to the first experimental explosion of an atomic bomb, which took place near Alamogordo, New Mexico, on the very same day.

The Wabash River Boat Club leased a portion of the park from the city in the 1920s and 1930s. Most of the land for the park was given to the city in 1916 by Crawford and Edward Fairbanks in memory of their father, Henry Fairbanks, mayor of the city during the 1870s.

280. Two riverboats, the *Reliance* and the *Reliable*, are shown near the Wabash Avenue bridge in 1929. These boats provided many hours of excursion pleasure for high school graduating classes and other local groups.

281. Swimmers and trees frame this June 1942 scene at the Izaak Walton Beach, west of the river in Sugar Creek Township.
   The Terre Haute Chapter of the Izaak Walton League was organized in 1923 at the Knights of Pythias temple. In 1928 the group secured 140 acres just north of West Terre Haute, and the north gravel pit became Walton Lake.

282. All ages waited for the circus to come to town. The Bays Brothers Circus arrived on Monday, June 24, 1935, for a noon parade and a "one day only" production at 25th Street and Wabash Avenue. Children's tickets were 10¢ each.

283. Boys play hockey at Memorial Park in 1940, where the sunken athletic field was flooded for skating in the winter. The park, located at 1500 N. 4th Street, was the scene of a ceremony conducted by veterans each Memorial Day.

284. This barefoot boy is waiting for a bite at the Fishing Rodeo at the Cow Pond, Brown Avenue and Ohio Street, in August 1949.

285. What boy or girl did not want to go to Deming Park for a pony ride in the 1940s?

The 155 acres for the park were acquired in 1921 with funds provided by Demas Deming. Some of the money was earmarked for the extension of Ohio Boulevard and Parkway through Deming's property from S. 25th Street to the park.

286. William Henry Harrison built Fort Harrison in 1811, and Zachary Taylor later commanded it. Both men became President of the United States. Not in their wildest dreams could they have pictured the beautiful facilities of the Fort Harrison Club, pictured here. Later, the Elks Country Club was also built on the site of the fort.

287. In 1950 golfers enjoy a Fourth of July match at the Phoenix Country Club, formerly the site of the Country Club of Terre Haute. The Phoenix was organized in 1899 and maintained a building (now the Labor Temple) for many years at S. 5th and Walnut streets.

288. A style show of old-fashioned bathing suits marks the opening season of the swimming pool at the Country Club of Terre Haute. Founded near the end of the century, the club was located east of Highland Lawn Cemetery before its move to Allendale in the early 1920s.

289. Rea Park, the city's first municipal golf course, was the gift of William S. Rea. It opened on August 1, 1925. The clubhouse, for which Mrs. Geraldine Rea donated $60,000, was constructed in 1925 and is shown here ten years later.

290. The Malleables win the Annual City Baseball Championship at Athletic Park in 1920. Twelve teams, including this winning team sponsored by the Terre Haute Malleable Corp., played in the series.

291. Fans filled the Indiana State gymnasium at N. 7th and Eagle streets in 1945 to see the champions of the Golden Gloves tournament crowned. The four-night contest, sponsored by the Tribune-Star Publishing Co., matched 123 contestants. Indiana State and the Boys Club tied for team honors; the local winners went on to the Tournament of Champions in Chicago.

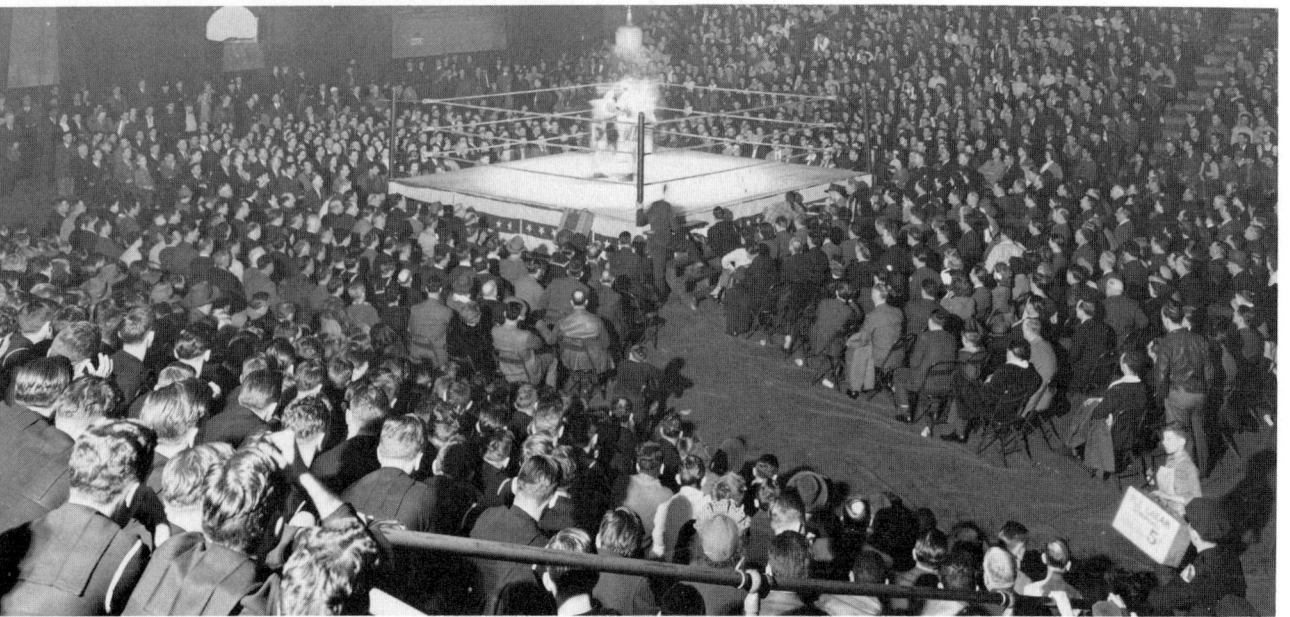

292. The Four-cornered Race Track, located at Wabash and Brown avenues, where Memorial Stadium is now, opened in 1887. It was used as the Terre Haute Mile Track until 1910, when the track was cut to a half-mile. Famous horses, including Axtell and Nancy Hanks, set records there.

293. The Terre Haute Phillies drew a large crowd of fans to Memorial Stadium for this night baseball game in 1948. The Phillies were preceded by the Terre Haute Baseball Club (first the Tots, then the Huts), a member of the Three-I League. The teams played from 1901 to 1937, first at the Terre Haute Ball Park at 27th Street and Wabash Avenue, and beginning in 1925, at Memorial Stadium.

The Phillies stayed from 1946 until 1955, when the Terre Haute Huts, a Detroit Tigers farm club, took over local baseball action. The Huts played all of the 1955 and half of the 1956 season.

294. Memorial Stadium was constructed on the site of the old fairgrounds in memory of the "boys who served in the World War." The first sporting event was the Garfield-Wiley football game, played on Thanksgiving Day, 1924. The official opening was May 4, 1925, and the following day 9,000 fans watched the Terre Haute Tots and the Peoria Tractors play ball. The stadium became an Indiana State University football facility in 1970.

295. The country was in the middle of the Great Depression in 1935, but some families managed to have a few nickels and dimes for the county fair on the stadium grounds. The hot air balloon on the left seems to have drawn the public away from the rides and tents. Billboard advertisers include Carl Wolf Clothing, McMillan Sporting Goods, Toastmaster Bread, Coca Cola, Terre Haute Pure Milk and Ice Cream Co., and Cook's Beer.

296. The last county fair was held at Memorial Stadium in 1949. This photograph shows the construction of the grandstand at the present Vigo County Fairgrounds, south of the city on U.S. 41, in August 1950.

297. 1946

298. 1944

County Fair Time

The products of the skills and labors of the rural population have been exhibited at Vigo County Fairs since the early 1850s.

299. 1947

300. 1949

301. Members of the Motorcycle Club in West Terre Haute gather for a photograph on October 23, 1949.

302. Five thousand people attend the Fifth Annual Soap Box Derby sponsored by Downtown Chevrolet and the Tribune-Star Publishing Co. on July 21, 1940. Thirty-five boys, eleven to fifteen years old, competed on Hauger Hill, 14.7 miles south of the city on Highway 63. Bud Fox, 13, was the winner.

303. Kids of all ages were entranced by James M. (Jimmie) Trimble's sleight of hand tricks. A sign painter by trade, he was well known for his magic shows. He served as president of the International Association of Magicians and showed his bag of tricks nationwide. Trimble was born in 1892 and died in 1971.

304. Presenting "Brown and Schomer—the Boys with the Feet that Talk in a Refined Singing and Dancing Act." After entertaining audiences on the vaudeville circuit for five years, the act broke up in 1909, and William Schomer opened a dancing school in Terre Haute. During his career, he also managed the Elm Grove Pavilion, the Summer Gardens, and the Trianon Dance Hall.

305. The Hippodrome Theatre was built in 1915 with seating for 1,000 vaudeville patrons. It later became the Wabash Movie House. The building was purchased in 1956 from the Wabash Theaters Corp. by the Scottish Rite, Valley of Terre Haute, for a new permanent cathedral.

306. *It Happens Every Spring* is the main feature at the Indiana Theatre, on the southwest corner of S. 7th and Ohio streets on July 12, 1949. The theatre opened in 1922 with a seating capacity of 2,000 for silent movies and vaudeville shows. Designed by John Eberson, it was reported to be one of the finest theatres in the country.

307. Admission to "Highclass Pictures RCA Perfect Sound" is 10¢ at the Fountain Theatre, 422 Wabash Avenue, in 1933. Note the NRA eagle and Mickey Mouse signs to the left of the box office.

In 1934 there were eight downtown theatres: American, Fountain, Grand, Hippodrome, Indiana, Liberty, Orpheum, and Savoy. Neighborhood movie houses included the Swan (Twelve Points), Little Virginia (1472 Locust Street) and the Lyceum (1235 Wabash Avenue).

308. The movie *Gone with the Wind* drew crowds wherever it appeared. In Terre Haute the place was the Grand Opera House, the year 1941.

Built in 1897–98 with a seating capacity of 1,500, the theatre portion of the building faced Cherry Street although the main entrance was off N. 7th Street.

309. and 310. Couples competed in this Jitterbug Contest at the Trianon in August 1941. The popular Trianon Dance Hall was located at 2831 Wabash Avenue.

311. Women and girls model the latest in 1916 fashions.

312. Members of Shirley Armstrong's Melody Misses, shown here in 1936, were Virginia Minar, Ethel Dahl, Shirley Armstrong, Betty Stultz, and Ruth Tranbarger.

313. Jimmy Adami's Orchestra played at the Terre Haute House Mayflower Room on September 29, 1946. This beautiful room was added to the east side of the building after the hotel was constructed. The mural depicting the landing of the *Mayflower* was familiar to the thousands who dined and danced there.

314. "Say cheese." The Jaycees sponsor this beauty contest in June 1946. The organization, chartered in 1936, was one of the first six chapters in Indiana.

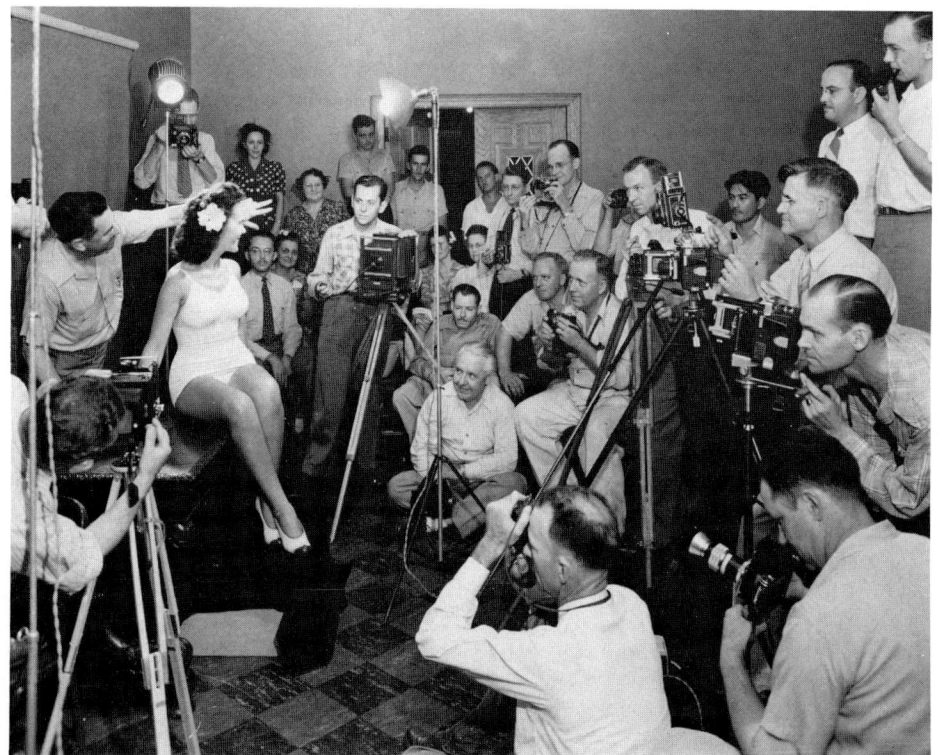

315. Willard Martin shares his camera expertise with the members of the Terre Haute Camera Club in August 1944. Miss Jane Scott is the model.

The Local Media

Local Wabash Valley events were first recorded by the Vincennes *Western Sun* in 1807. The newspaper business began in Terre Haute with the publication of the *Western Register and Terre Haute Advertiser* in 1823. These papers and their successors have given the community a detailed record of local people and events.

The first Terre Haute radio station began broadcasting more than a century later; local telecasting was not to arrive until the second half of this century.

Newspapers

1900	1925	1950
Terre Haute *Express*	*Saturday Spectator*	*Saturday Spectator*
Terre Haute *Gazette*	Terre Haute *Post*	Terre Haute *Advocate*
Terre Haute *Journal* (German)	Terre Haute *Star*	(labor)
Terre Haute *Tribune*	Terre Haute *Tribune*	Terre Haute *Star*
Terre Haute *Weekly News*		Terre Haute *Tribune*

316. "Read all about it!"
Earl Wetzel was a well-known newspaper peddler. The streets and the depots were his territory. He rarely missed a train's arrival. He is pictured here at 7th Street and Wabash Avenue during the 1920s. The Terre Haute Trust Co. building (later the Merchants National Bank) is in the background.

317. Flood waters in 1943 do not prevent the *Tribune* from being delivered to West Terre Haute subscribers. These householders hardly needed to read the headline: "River at an All-Time High."

318. Morning comes early to these *Star* carriers at the S. 13th and Crawford streets substation in 1946. The first daily newspaper in Terre Haute was the Wabash *Daily Express* (1841). It became the Terre Haute *Daily Express* and then the Terre Haute *Morning Star* in 1903. The *Star* was sold to the *Tribune* in 1931.

319. William E. Cronin was a long time editor of the Terre Haute *Tribune*. The paper was first published in 1894. Its predecessor was the Terre Haute *Gazette*, established in 1869.

320. Alonzo "Cap" Duddleston was one of the editors of the *Saturday Spectator*. Founded by Don Nixon in 1904, the paper was a local weekly tradition until 1980.

321. Students discovered the work behind the printed page in the Tribune-Star Publishing Co. composing room in 1948.

322. Si and Ezra, pictured in the barnyard in 1935, were the popular characters of an early WBOW radio show. In real life they were Guy Slover and Gene Morgan.
  The first radio station in the area, Rose Polytechnic Institute's WRPI, went on the air in 1927. The next year the call letters were changed to WBOW.

323. WTHI began broadcasting in January 1948, from 120 S. 7th Street. At the end of that year the station was purchased by Anton Hulman, Jr. Television shows were not produced locally until 1954.

324. Burl Ives and Wee Bonnie Baker of "Oh, Johnny, Oh" fame are the center of attraction in this WBOW group in 1942.

325., 326., and 327. During the early 1920s the Liberty Theatre featured a local newsreel. The photograph above shows the DeVry 35 mm camera placed to "shoot" a freshly cut bee tree.

From 1928 until 1979 a rotogravure section was part of each Sunday edition of the Tribune Star Publishing Co. During that entire period, Ken Martin (left) made many of the "photos for the rotos." The *Sunday Pictorial Rotogravure* mirrored the small-town aspect of the city during those years.

Willard C. Martin, right, made the first "movies" of Terre Haute from the air.

Photo Credits

328. Frank J. Martin, 1870–1933, founder of Martins Photo Shop.

Martins Photo Shop: cover photo, p. 3, p. 7, p. 9, illus. 3–7, 9, 10, 12, 14–17, 19–33, 37–45, 48, 52, 54–59, 63, 64, 66, 68–75, 78, 80, 84, 89, 91, 95, 96 (and insert), 98, 100, 102–104, 106–10, 112–14, 116–26, 128, 131, 132, 136–42, 144, 146–65, 168, 176, 180, 181, 186, 187, 190–92, 195, 196, 199–205, 208, 209, 211–13, 216, 217, 220–24, 226, 228–34, 237, 238, 240, 244, 249–52, 254, 256, 257, 259–67, 269, 271, 273–75, 278–82, 284, 286, 287, 290–303, 306–11, 313–28
Martin Photo, Forrest Sherer Agency, Inc., collection: p. 5
Vigo County Historical Society collection: p. 8, illus. 1, 2, 8, 11, 13, 18, 34–36, 46, 47, 49–51, 61, 62, 65, 67, 76, 77, 82, 85–88, 90, 94, 97, 99, 101, 105, 111, 133, 134, 143, 145, 166, 169–73, 175, 177–79, 182–84, 188, 189, 193, 194, 197, 206, 207, 210, 214, 215, 218, 219, 236, 239, 243, 246–48, 268, 276, 277, 288, 304, 312
Turner Coaches, Inc., collection: illus. 53
Martin Photos, Vigo County Historical Society collection: illus. 60, 129, 289, 305
Terre Haute Savings Bank collection: illus. 79
R. Hape Photos, Vigo County Historical Society collection: illus. 81, 258, 272, 283, 285
Indiana State Bank collection: illus. 83
Martin Photo, Ermisch Cleaners and Shirt Laundry collection: illus. 92
Paige's Music collection: illus. 93
General Housewares Corp. collection: illus. 115
Robert Prox collection: illus. 127
IMC collection: illus. 130
Eugene V. Debs Foundation, Inc., collection: illus. 135
Robert Johnson collection: illus. 167
Floyd Mitchell collection: illus. 174
Martin Photo, Pat Calvert collection: illus. 185
Martin Photo, Thomas Funeral Home collection: illus. 198
Martin Photo, Vigo County Public Library collection: illus. 225
Martin Photo, Indiana Business College collection: illus. 227
Leon Miller collection: illus. 235
Myrtle Fuller collection: illus. 241
Leo Deming Photo, Gibault School for Boys collection: illus. 242
Martin Photo, Swope Art Gallery collection: illus. 245
J. C. Rutledge collection: illus. 253
Martin Photo, St. George's Orthodox Church collection: illus. 255
Goodwill Industries collection: illus. 270

Index

Adami, Jimmy, Orchestra, 119
Aesculapian Society of the Wabash Valley, 82
agriculture, 30–31
airplanes, 28
Allen Chapel, 98
Alvey Feed and Poultry Co., 43
American Bus Lines, 27
American Can Co., 49
American Car and Foundry Co., 47
American Legion, 65, 66
American Red Cross, 57, 105
Anshutz, Frank P. and Wade, dentists, 16
Armstrong, Shirley, 119
Associated Physicians & Surgeons Clinic, 98
Athletic Park, 111
automobile dealers, 43
automobiles, 26
aviation commissioners, 29
Axtell, 112

B.P.O.E. *See* Elks Lodge #86
Baker, Wee Bonnie, 123
Ball, Caroline Peddle, 95
banks, 35, 36. *See also* individual names of banks
Barbazette, John, 46
Barnes, Dr. James, 97
Bartruff, Pauline, 61, 104
baseball, 111, 112
Baur, Mrs. Oscar, 97
Bays Bros. Circus, 108
Beal, Dorel, 42
Beck Optical, 15
Beecher, Mayor Sam, 99
Bell Telephone, 45
Best Theatre, 97
Bidaman, Mayor Frank, 68
Biel, Fred J., Cigar Factory, 37
Big Four Depot, 24, 63
Big Four Railroad, 23
Blackhawk, 32
Blackhawk School, 92
Bledsoe, Walter, Co. Mine, 33
Bon Ton Food Shoppe, 42
Bowers Black and White Cab Co., 26
Boys Club, 105, 111

Boy Scouts, 104
Braden, Forrest, 12
bridge (Wabash River), 21, 22, 107
Browder, Earl, 54, 62
Brown and Schomer, 116
Brown, Madam Edith, 69
Bryant, Dr. Will, 97
Buckingham, Mayor Frank, 68
buses (city), 16, 27
buses (school), 92
business and industry, 34–53. *See also* individual names of businesses and industries
business schools, 88

Calvary Methodist Church, 60, 103
Carnegis, George, 16
Carpenters Local #133, 14
Casey, George, 28
Centenary Church, 98
Central Park & Service, 21
Chalos, John, 16
Chalos, Mayor Pete, 16
Chamber of Commerce, 53
Champagne Velvet Beer, 48
Chauncey Rose Junior High School, 91
Chauncey Rose School, 101
Child Welfare Association, 105
Children's Theatre, 97
Church of the Immaculate Conception, 84
churches, 98–100. *See also* individual names of churches
Citizens Trust Co., 36
City Hall (new), 11, 60
City Hall (old), 11
City Market, 11
Civil Defense, 65
Clabber Girl Baking Powder, 41
Clara Fairbanks Home for Aged Women, 101
Coal Bluff, 32
coal mining, 32, 51
colleges and universities, 84–88. *See also* individual names of colleges
Collett, Josephus, 106
Collett Park, 106
Collins, H. Arth, 21
Colored Day Nursery, 105
Colored Orphans Home, 60
Columbian Enameling & Stamping Co., 47, 62
Columbian Laundry Co., 39
Commercial Club, 34, 53
Commercial Solvents Co., 52
Community Chest, 105
Community Fund Agencies, 105
Community Theatre, 97
Conrail, 23
corruption (political), 68
Coudert, Amelia Kussner, 95

Country Club of Terre Haute, 110
Courthouse, Vigo County, 8, 12
Cox, B. G., 31
Cox, Paul S., 29
Crawford, Mary Sinclair, 94
Crescent Theatre, 16
Cronin, William E., 122
Cross, Dolph, 11

Dahl, Ethel, 119
Danner, William J., Dry Goods Store, 79
Darwin Ferry, 71
Davis Gardens, 30
Debs, Eugene V., 14, 54, 55
Deming, Demas, 109
Deming Hotel, 26
Deming Park, 80, 109
department stores, 17, 20
Depression, 60, 61
Dewees, Major George W., 76
dime stores, 17
Dinkel, Ralph C., 12
Dixie Bee Line, 22
Dollar Day, 17
"Doodlebug," 32
Downtown Chevrolet, 43, 115
Dreiser, Theodore, 96
Dresser, Paul, 96
Dresser, Paul, Memorial, 60
Dresser Field, 22, 28, 29
Dresser School, 60, 94
drugstores, 44
Duddleston, Alonzo, 122
DuPont Powder Mill explosion, 74
DuPont Snow Hill Mine #3, 33

Early, Samuel F., residence, 103
Edgewood Stock Farm, 31
Ehrmann, Max, 70, 96
Ehrmann Manufacturing Co., 15
Elks Country Club, 110
Elks Lodge #86, 102
Elm Grove Pavilion, 116
Emeline Fairbanks Memorial Library, 88, 95
Empire Theatre, 14
Ermisch Dyeing and Cleaning Co., 39

fair. *See* Vigo County Fair
Fairbanks, Crawford, 88, 107
Fairbanks, Edward, 107
Fairbanks, Henry, 107
Fairbanks Block, 14
Fairbanks Park, 60, 103, 104, 108
Falber's Music, 15
Farmers Chapel Church, 73
Federal Building. *See* Post Office
Federal Prison, 13
Filbeck Hotel, 27

Fire Department (Terre Haute), 10, 12
First Baptist Church, 98
First Congregational Church, 105
First Methodist Church, 98
First Terre Haute Hungarian Society Park, 100
Fishing Rodeo, 109
Fitch, Harry E., 29, 55
floods, 80, 81, 121
Flora Gulick Boys Club. *See* Boys Club
Florence Crittenden Home, 105
florists, 45
Foltz, Don, 31
Fontanet, 32, 74
Forest Park, 106
Forest Park Mill, 30
Fort Harrison, 13
Fort Harrison Club, 110
Fort Harrison Country Club, 102
Fort Harrison Post No. 40, 66
Fort Harrison School, 92
Fountain Theatre, 117
Four-cornered Track, 117
Fowler Park, 71
Fox, Bud, 115
Fresh Air Mission, 105

gambling, 69
Garfield High School, 6, 60, 90, 113
Gartland Foundry Co., 51
Geckeler's, Gilbert, Wabash Fish Market, 21
general strike, 54, 62
Gerrish, Dr. Don, 75
Gerstmeyer High School, 85, 91
Gibault Home for Boys, 94
Giffel Body Co., 27
Gilbert, Curtis, 13
Gilkison, E. P. & Sons, 26
Gillis Drug Co., 15, 44
Girls Club of Terre Haute, 61
Girl Scouts, 71, 104
glass factories, 49
Glenn, Herschell, 44
Glenn Home, 101
Golden Gloves Tournament, 111
Goodwill Industries, 60, 103
Grand Opera House, 117
Grob, Rev. Theodore, 60, 103
grocery stores, 78
Grover Station, 32
Guerin, Mother Theodore, 84
Gulick, Flora Gilman, 105

Hansel, C. D., 30
Hansell Cigar Stand, 36
Harrison, Henry W., Carpet Weaving, 37
Hauck, George, Fish Market, 43
Hayman, Mort, 28

126

Hazledine, E. T., Machine and Architectural Iron Works, 38
Hazledine, Margaret, 23
Heminway Park, 104
Henley Bros. Florists, 45
Highland Iron and Steel Co., 34
Highland Lawn Cemetery, 101, 110
Highland School, 93
Hippodrome Theatre, 116
Historical Museum of the Wabash Valley, 95
Home Packing Co., 46, 61
Honey Creek, 71
Honey Creek Square, 31
Hooks Drugs, 67
House, George, 105
Hudnut Co., 37
Hudson residence, 95
Hulman, Anton, Jr., 17, 29, 41, 53, 123
Hulman Field, 29, 80
Hulman, Francis, 41
Hulman & Co., 41
Hulman, Herman, 34, 83
Hungarian Hall, 100

immigrants, 100
Indian Refining Co. Station, 43
Indiana Gas and Chemical Corp., 51
Indiana Loan Co., 16
Indiana Savings Loan and Building Association, 36
Indiana State Bank, 36
Indiana State Normal School, 84
Indiana State Teachers College, 60, 62, 65, 86, 87
Indiana State University, 86, 102, 113
Indiana Theatre, 97, 117
industry and business, 34–53. See also individual names of businesses and industries
International Minerals & Chemical Corp., 52
interurbans, 22, 25, 27
Irishman's Covered Bridge, 71
Ives, Burl, 123
Izaak Walton Beach, 108
Izaak Walton League, 108

jail (Vigo County), 12
James, Harley, Livery Stable, 79
Jaycees, 62, 120
Jenckes, Virginia, 11
Jenckes farm, 101
Johnson Brothers (Louis, Harry, Julius, Clarence), 28
Judson, Billy, residence, 74

Kaufman Block, 16
Kerman Grotto, 94
Kinser, Thomas, residence, 102
Kitchell, Joseph, 10
Kessel, Mrs. Harry, 31

Kibler's Feed Mill, 72
King, Bertha Pratt, 94
King Classical School, 94
King Lem Inn Cafe, 15
Klatte farm, 101
K-Mart Shopping Center, 101
Knights of Columbus, 94, 102
Knights of Pythias Temple, 108
Krach, Ted, Marathon Filling Station, 21
Kresge, S. S., 17
Krietenstein Paint & Glass Co., 44
Krietenstein Post #104, 65
Ku Klux Klan, 54
Kussner, Amelia. See Coudert, Amelia Kussner

Labor Temple, 110
Laboratory School, 104
Lease Brothers Billiard Hall, 4
Levi, Simon, Dry Goods and Notions, 15
Liberty Theatre, 124
Light, Ed, Saloon, 59
Light, Frances J., Millinery Shop, 42
Light House Mission, 61, 105
Lions Club, 105
Lost Creek Township School, 92
Louden Packing Co., 30

M A B Paints, 47
McFall, John, 77
McFall, John (founder Home Packing Co.), 46
McFall, Robert, 46
McGurk, Mrs. H. L., 104
McKeen Bank Building, 34
McKeen Block, 14
McMillan, Mayor Vern, 29, 69
McNeal, Miles, 106
Mahaney, Patsy, Confectionary, 16
Markle Mill, 33
Marshall, B. V., 46
Marshall, Leonard, 29
Martin, Frank, 3, 75, 125
Martin, Kenneth, 45, 124
Martin, Stewart, 45
Martin, Willard, 45, 120, 124
Martins Photo Shop, 8, 16, 45
Masonic Temple, 102
Masons, 102
Maumee Collieries, 33
Mayer, Anton, 48
Mayflower Room, 119
Mayors (Terre Haute), 11
Melody Misses, 119
Memorial Hall, 34
Memorial Park, 109
Memorial Stadium, 112, 113
Merchants Distillery, 48
Merchants National Bank, 35, 121

Mercury (statue), 34
Methodist Temple, 98
Miller Bros. Bakery, 66
Miller-Parrott Baking Co., 61, 66
Miller, Victor, 66
millinery shops, 42
Minar, Virginia, 119
Miners' picnic, 32
mining. See coal mining
Minshall home, 27
Mogger, Mathias, 48
Monterey Land Co., 36
Moore, Ted, 105
More Park, 31
Morgan, Gene, 123
Morris, Arthur, 73
Mueller, Harry, 29
Musick, Harry, 28
Myer, Herman, and family, 26
Myers, Moses, 76

Nancy Hanks, 112
National Road, 22
Nattkemper, Otto, 10
Nevins Township, 31, 74
New York Central Railroad, 23
Newlin-Johnson Real Estate, 36
newspapers, 121–122
Nichols, Lex, 105
Nixon, Don, 122
Normal Training School, 86
North Terre Haute Feed Store, 86

Oakley Economy Stores, 78
Oakley, Hollie and Anna, 104
Opera House Block, 102
Optimist Club, 20
Otter Creek, 106
Otter Creek Township, 33
Otter Creek Township Volunteer Fire Department, 75
Overland motor car, 38

Paige, W. H., & Co., 40
Paitson Brothers (Edward, Jr., Walter, Fred, Stanley, Robert), 78
parades, 14, 87
parks. See individual names of parks
Paul Cox Field, 29
penitentiary. See Federal Prison
Penn Central Railroad, 23
Pennsylvania Railroad, 23
Pfizer Co., 52, 63
Phillips, Walter, 79
Phyllis Wheatley Association, 105
Phoenix Country Club, 110
Pierson Township, 92
Pillsbury Co., 49

Pittman, Sterling, 21
Police Department (Terre Haute), 11, 12
population (Terre Haute and Vigo County), 10
Porter, Lt. James W., 12
Post Office, 13
Prairie City Bank Building, 35
Prairie Creek, 74
Prairie House, 17
Prairieton General Store, 72
Prairieton Township, 72
Preston, Nathaniel, 76
Preston House, 76
prison. See Federal Prison
Prohibition, 59
prostitution, 69
Providence Hospital, 83
Prox, Frank, Co., 51
Prox, Robert, 29
Public Health Nursing Association, 105
Punch, 37
PWA projects, 11, 60

Quaker Maid, 52, 61

radio, 121, 123
railroad accidents, 66
railroads, 22–24
Ray, W. W., 46
Rea, Geraldine, 110
Rea, William, 110
Rea Park, 110
Red Cross. See American Red Cross
Riley Masonic Lodge Building, 102
Riley Township School Building, 60
Roberts, Donn, 68
Root, Chapman, 49
Root Dry Goods Co., 40
Root Glass Co., 49
Rose Aid Home, 101
Rose, Chauncey, 17, 83, 85
Rose, Chauncey, Memorial, 60
Rose Dispensary, 82, 83
Rose-Hulman Institute of Technology, 85
Rose Ladies Aid Society, 101
Rose Old Ladies Home, 105
Rose Orphans Home, 101
Rose Polytechnic Institute, 56, 84, 85, 91, 123
rotogravure, 67, 124
Royse, James S., 57
rural life, 71–75
Ryan, Patrolman Edward M., 12

Sage-Robinson-Nagel home, 95
St. Agnes Hall, 83
St. Andrew Roumanian Orthodox Church, 100
St. Anthony's Hospital, 82, 83

St. Benedict Church, 99
St. George Orthodox Church, 99
St. Joseph Church, 99
St. Mary-of-the-Woods College, 84
St. Mary's Female Institute, 84
Salvation Army, 64
Saturday Spectator, 122
Sayre, Edwin, Jr., Bicycle Shop, 43
Saxon Mine, 33
Schomer, William, 116
schools, 89–94. *See also* individual names of schools
Scofield Optical, 16
Scott, Jane, 120
Scottish Rite, 116
Scudder, Janet, 95
Shandy, Jerome, 29
Shandy's Court House Pharmacy, 44
Sherer, Forrest, 5
Sheriff (Vigo County), 12
Showalter's Books, 15
Si and Ezra, 123
Silver's Specialty Shop, 21
Sisters of Providence, 84
Slover, Guy, 123
Smith-Alsop Paint and Varnish Co., 47
Soap Box Derby, 115
Society for Organizing Charity, 105
Soldiers and Sailors Monument, 10
Standard Wheel Company, 38
Starkey, Chauncey, 25
State Bank of Indiana, 34, 35
Steeg Park, 66
Stran Steel, 47
Strawberry Hill, 77
street cars, 15, 16, 25, 27, 106
strip mining, 32
Strupp Dental Laboratory, 16
Stuempfle & Welte's Washington Saloon, 15
Stultz, Betty, 119
Sugar Creek Township, 80, 108
Summer Gardens, 116
Swafford, Dr. B. F., 82
Swander, John H., 79
Swope Art Gallery, 95
Sycamore Building, 36

Taylorville, 80, 81
Taylorville School, 94
Temple B'nai Abraham, 100
Temple Israel, 100
Terminal Arcade, 25, 27
telephones, 45
Terre Haute Airways, Inc., 28
Terre Haute Ball Park, 112
Terre Haute Brewing Co., 48, 59
Terre Haute Boys Club. *See* Boys Club
Terre Haute Camera Club, 120

Terre Haute Commercial College, 88
Terre Haute Concrete Supply Corp., 50
Terre Haute First National Bank, 35
Terre Haute Gravel Co., 50
Terre Haute High School, 89
Terre Haute House, 15, 17, 119
Terre Haute Huts, 112
Terre Haute Indianapolis and Eastern Traction Co., 25
Terre Haute Land Company, 10
Terre Haute Library Association, 88
Terre Haute Lodge #19, F. and A.M., 102
Terre Haute Malleable Corp., 51, 111
Terre Haute National Bank and Trust Co., 35
Terre Haute Phillies, 112
Terre Haute Regional Hospital, 83
Terre Haute Sanitarium, 82
Terre Haute Savings Bank, 35
Terre Haute Star, 121
Terre Haute Symphony, 97
Terre Haute Tots, 112, 113
Terre Haute Traction and Light Co., 25
Terre Haute Tribune, 121
Terre Haute Trust Co., 35, 57, 121
Terre Haute Vitrified Brick Works, 50
Tetzel, Ed, 38
theatres, 117. *See also* individual names of theatres
Thomas, C. B. and Lettie May, 79
Thomas, Ray, 29
Thomas Funeral Home, 79
Three-I League, 112
tornadoes, 80
Torner Community House, 61
Townsley, Madge Polk, 97
Tranbarger, Ruth, 119
transportation, 22–29
Tribune Building, 4
Tribune Publishing Co., 4
Tribune-Star Publishing Co., 67, 111, 115, 122, 124
Trianon Dance Hall, 116, 118
Trierweiler, Sheriff John, 12
Trimble, James (Jimmie), 116
Tucker, Ralph, 11, 27
Tune Building, 102
Turner, Charles, 27
Twelve Points, 16, 79, 90
Twelve Points Dry Goods Co., 79

Union Consolidated Bus Terminal, 27
Union Depot, 15, 24, 50, 56
Union Hospital, 82
United Cigar Co., 16
United Hebrew Congregation, 100
Universalist Church, 103

Varieties Theatre, 15

Vendel, William, 10
Vigo, Francis, 10
Vigo County Fair, 113, 114
Vigo County Fairgrounds, 113
Vigo County Historical Society, 71, 95
Vigo County Infirmary, 60
Vigo County Medical Society, 82
Vigo County Public Library, 88, 89, 98
Vigo County School Corporation, 92
Vigo County Welfare Department, 101
Vigo Ice and Cold Storage Co., 46
Vigo Ordinance, 63
Volunteers of America, 105
Voorhees School, 99

Wabash Avenue, cover photo, 14, 21
Wabash River, 4, 22, 76
Wabash River Boat Club, 107
Wabash Senior Citizens Center, 100
Wabash Theatre, 116
Wabash Valley Bus Line, 27
Wabash Valley Council of Boy Scouts. *See* Boy Scouts
Warren Park, 31
Washington School, 93
WBOW, 123
Weinstein, Dr. L. J., 82
Weldin Talley Memorial Playhouse, 97
Well Child Clinic, 93
Western Discount Co., 36
Western Indiana Gravel Co., 50
Western Register and Terre Haute Advertiser, 121
Westminster Village, 30
West Terre Haute, 50, 72, 78, 108, 115
West Terre Haute auditorium, 60
West Terre Haute Motorcycle Club, 115
Wetzel, Earl, 121
Wiley, W. H., 89, 93
Wiley High School, 89, 113
Wilson, Gilbert, 95
Woman's Department Club, 27, 95
Women's Army Auxiliary Corps (WAAC), 65
Women's Organization of Retail Druggists, 101
World War I, 55–56
World War II, 63–67
WPA projects, 94
WRPI, 123
WTHI, 123

Yellow Cab Co., 15
YMCA, 103
YWCA, 103

Zwerner, Ernest L., 67